Her Name Shall Remain Unforgotten

A child in the heart of the genocide

MARION DEICHMANN

MARGATE, NEW JERSEY

Copyright © 2017 by Marion Deichmann

All rights reserved. No part of this book may be used or reproduced in any manner, electronic or mechanical, including photocopying, recording or by any information storage and retrieval system, or otherwise, without written permission from the author.

Margate, New Jersey 08402
609-487-9000
ComteQpublishing.com

ISBN 978-1-941501-26-9

Printed in the United States of America

Acknowledgments

This book has been made possible with the help in translating from the French by friends W. Allen, P. McCarey and my daughter S. Debossu.

Table of contents

I -	Introduction	7
II -	Prologue	9
	Becoming a citizen of the world	9
III -	Family history: the Aron genealogy	13
IV -	Early childhood in Germany (1932 -1934)	21
	Visits with my grandparents in Saarbrücken (1934 – 1938)	21
V -	Luxembourg (1934 -1940)	27
VI -	France, September 1940	39
VII -	Paris from 1940 to July 1942	41
	Arrival (1940 – 1941)	41
	Paris, race laws and restrictions (1941 and early 1942)	50
	1942 (January to July): a black year	53
	The noose tightens for the Jews	54
	The Final Solution	56
	Preparation for the mass arrests of 16 and 17 July 1942	56
VIII -	The Arrests, the « Rafle du Vel d'Hiv » Thursday 16 July 1942	59
IX -	Drancy	61
	My mother's fate	61
X -	Auschwitz	65
XI -	Wandering	67
XII -	Normandy, February or March 1943 to December 1944	105
	Exodus to the farm (June – August 1944)	111

XIII -	Paris (1945 – 1947)	119
XIV -	Sailing to New York… and back to France (September 1947 - December 1953)	135
XV -	My life in America	149
XVI -	Reunion with my father	151
XVII -	Epilogue	157
XVIII -	Addenda	161
	1. The "Righteous of the Nations" title given to the Parignys.	161
	2. A "Stolperstein" for my mother in 2016	162
	3. Montréal, Canada with Hélène 2016-17	163
XIX -	Annexes	165
	1. History of the Jews of the Sarre region (Saarland) -	165
	2. The thirteen Bocks: the identity and fate of the children of a Judeo-Protestant couple	167
	3. Comparative history	170
XX -	Bibliography	175

I - Introduction

To my children, to my grandchildren

The time has come when I am able to tell my story. A time when I can tell you about my mother. It has been so long since she left… It was in 1942, during the Second World War, the years when our planet was fire and blood. I would like to convey to you an intangible world, a world that no longer exists, a world destroyed by the war.

I've chosen to tell my story in French, the language of reason, and my age of reason, of coming of age! German, my mother tongue, was then the language of hate, the language in which one shouts and kills, in which German Jews were hounded. And yet I spoke only German to my mother, except in public places in France, when we couldn't betray our origins, when we had to hide our identities. Then we spoke in recently acquired French. I called my mother "*mutti*" or "mama", depending on the occasion or the context. These two languages merge in my memory. Impressed onto the depths of my soul still remain the image of her face, the way she moved, the colors of her clothes. She was at the same time my mother, father, country, anchor. Then one summer day it was all swept away and it was in quite another world that I was to grow up.

In front of my eyes, the eyes of a child, she was taken away from me one morning. Then there was a train, a convoy that left from Drancy, then the Auschwitz concentration camp, and then, and then, and then…A gas chamber, blazes and a pile of ashes mixed with piles of other ashes. Her, and not me. Why?

An abyss that separates me from my mother, created by the evils of "humanity". A bottomless abyss across which, one day at a time, I had to build a bridge to live. Without really knowing why. A solitude inhabited by my mother. Memory is what remains, but it is the feelings experienced that give the keys to the apprenticeship of becoming a person.

Research into my mother's death was only possible sixty years after the facts. Only recently did I dare to write to Auschwitz to request a death certificate. The reply I received from Poland was like a second death: upon arrival at the camp my mother was neither registered nor tattooed. She was sent directly to the gas chamber where she choked to death by gas and then was engulfed in flames. In the eyes of the demons of industrialized murder she no longer deserved to live. I will perhaps never stop mourning my mother's death. This is her resting place.

II - Prologue

I am a Syrian, what is so surprising?
Stranger, man has only one homeland, the world;
The same chaos created all the mortals.

Meleagre
Greek poet IInd Century B.C.

Becoming a citizen of the world

In 2010, on the recommendation of the French Ministry for Immigration, there was a debate on the French national identity. A pamphlet was sent to all regional capital cities: "What is a true Frenchman? ". This brought back memories of very terrible times.

I was born in Germany on 18 November 1932. Hitler came to power on 30 January 1933. I was barely three years old when the Third Reich's race laws were introduced, on 15 September 1935. All German Jews lost first their civil rights and then finally their nationality was revoked. We were to become stateless. And so I lived without a nationality. I was a "refugee coming from Germany" and this is how I lived in Luxembourg, France and then in the United States. I was finally naturalized an American citizen in 1961. It was a grand ceremony and gave me a very great sense of security. It also simplified the official side of life!

Being stateless raised suspicion among the outside world. But this didn't truly affect me. I've always felt "beyond norms". I have lived in France for so long, in particular during the crucial adolescent years, that I identify with French culture. But I am in fact a mixture of cultures,

German, French and American, with my family's Jewish historical heritage as foundation. German by birth, French in my heart, passionate believer in American-style democracy, but Godless... And Jewish to the outside world .... What a strange amalgam!

Race laws made me a Jew banished from my own country. But as I hadn't received a religious education, it didn't occur to me that wearing a distinctive yellow Star of David on my clothes meant that I belonged to a group that was different from the others. Being forced to wear this badge meant being excluded, humiliated, and above all in danger of death, of being hunted like an animal. I lived in fear for five long years.

There is nothing comparable to the extermination of European Jews in the twentieth century. And yet in the Germany of the 18th, 19th, and early 20th centuries Jews could truly be both German and Jewish. The two identities were not mutually exclusive.

The philosophers of the Enlightenment, in particular Moses Mendelsohn (1729 – 86), laid the foundations for opposition to religious obscurantism, secrecy, in particular Judaism. Previously there had been Spinoza, a great philosopher who was excluded from the Jewish community. He maintained that the hate that Jews inspired was due in great part to their adherence to their religious rites. This hate went back, in his view, to the dawn of Christianity in Rome, for not only did the Jews not want to recognize Christ as God, but their customs also seemed incomprehensible to Christians. The Jewish minority was devoutly attached to its beliefs and the Christians felt this to be a threat.

I've always thought that, although they later became integrated, practicing Jews withdrew themselves from others to form their own communities - which today are called communitarianism. At the same time, I understand that they would have found the development of Catholicism difficult to comprehend, and were not able to convert to it. How difficult - if not impossible - it must be for practicing Jews to accept Jesus Christ as the Messiah. These are two different worlds in my opinion, with Protestantism falling somewhere in between the two.

It's in France, after the Revolution, that Louis XVI – who supported the emancipation of the Jews –ratified a law declaring Jews to be French citizens. Under the 1791 law, Jews became full French citizens.

In a Germany split into many small independent states, Jews did not yet benefit from civil rights. This came much later, in 1871, after the unification of Germany was complete. It was during this time that anti-Semitism started to spread and people begun to talk of "Aryans" and "Semites". There was an increase in virulent anti-Semitic propaganda in both Germany and France, the effects of which continued and intensified into the twentieth century. There were many theories put forward as to the origins of "races".

But the great majority of German Jews were assimilated into German culture. This is evidenced by mixed marriages, like that of my great grandparents and then their children, which were frequent in the nineteenth century. My grandfather, Isidor Aron, was a practicing Jew, but considered himself first to be German above all, and then Jewish.

Upon the creation of the Nazi Party in 1920 most Jews, as well as other Germans, thought that the "Brown Shirts" (SA) party could not last long. But anti-Semitism grew and manifested itself in different ways: biological, racial (exacerbated by the theories of the 19th century) and nationalistic. Darwin's writings were twisted and used for racist ends, and only Jews were targeted. Published works sought to demonstrate that the Jewish "race" was physically inferior. Hitler only had to seize power; everything was ready for him to carry out his plan….

As far as I am concerned, I am a Jew of the diaspora, and I also have some non-Jewish Protestant roots. For me this is important mostly for historical and genealogical reasons. I am a non-believer. A western homo sapiens.

After having been initiated into Catholicism during the war, I became non-believer in 1946, at the age of thirteen. I remember the moment: I was in fifth grade, and my friends and I were discussing religion, God and the existence of God. Many were believers but didn't go to church much. Some were non-believers, and it was around their ideas that I tended. I was not really a dissident, but I felt better without a particular religion and its God

It is History and my own personal history, not faith, which bind me to the Jewish people. It is the suffering I felt in my flesh, and the collective memory, that bind me to the Jewish people, not religious rites. At one time, being Jewish meant death. My mother was assassinated for the simple fact that she was Jewish.

III - Family history: the Aron genealogy

The Aron family had been settled in the Saar Basin (Saarland) for centuries. For the years before 1750, knowledge of Hebrew is needed to track down and read the texts on the gravestones, if any remain. We found the trace of Moses Aron, born in 1756 in Steinbach am Glan, some 30 kilometers from Homburg; he died in Homburg in 1800. (see family tree on p. 19)

Having arrived in the middle ages, the family had received permission to settle in Steinbach. They probably lived in the ghetto, a town within a town. Most Jews were poor and paid huge taxes. They were not allowed to exercise a profession. They were also prohibited from owning land. Thus they were mostly peddlers and traders in farm and agricultural products. Among the protected Jews of Homburg in 1790 were an actor, a musician, a horse trader, an innkeeper, a rabbi, a teacher and a pest controller.

The Aron family survived as it pleased the ruling classes or the Church, who expelled them or killed them whenever they needed a scapegoat. Jews were protected in certain royal or princely city-States. Then later expelled again. A large Jewish community existed in Furth in Bavaria from the 16th century, under the protection of the government of the ruling Prince. However their presence was forbidden in Nuremberg. The Bock family, on my grandmother's side, is originally from this region.

During the course of the following centuries, the spread of nationalistic and fascistic beliefs was such that the more Jews felt themselves to be German, the more the hostility, anti-Semitism and segregation increased. From the second half of the nineteenth century the majority of Jews felt that they were first and foremost German, and Jewish by religion; even religious Jews like my grandfather. Some 523,000 Jews lived in Germany in January 1933, barely 1% of the population. Of these, 80% had their roots in Germany. The remainder were immigrants.

At the end of the 19th century virulent tracts against the Jews were appearing - the expression "anti-Semitism" is German: "antisemitismus". This period represented the culmination of the persecution, pogroms and anti-Semitic teachings that a short time later was to lead a part of the human race into darkness.

Hitler was possessed by a hatred of the Jews. Like many in his entourage his racism knew no bounds. From 1920 onwards, from the creation of the Nazi Party, and after Hitler's putsch of 1923, most Jews thought that the party could not last, even less take power. Even those who had read "Mein Kampf" did not believe in it as a political force. For them Hitler's accession to power in January 1933 was merely a mistake of history.

My mother's family was among this group. We paid a very high human price for this error of judgment. But how could they, who had fought for Germany in the wars of 1870 and 1914, believe in this aberration? My great-grandfathers and grandfathers had all received medals!

When I talked to my father about the wars the Deichmanns had fought in, he told me that during a Nazi parade in the streets of Hoya, in 1934, my great-grandfather who was 87 years old, threw all his medals of the 1870-71 war in protest out of the window. His son, Ivan Deichmann, had fought at Verdun in the war of 1914-1918. He received the Medal of Honor – the Ehrenkreuz für Frontkämpfer - on 20 April 1934; five months before the Nuremberg race laws and four years before he was interned in Buchenwald.

Thirty-seven thousands of the 500,000 of the country's Jews left Germany from 1933 onwards. The majority moved to neighboring countries. My grandparents were subjected to violence starting in 1933, such as the smashing of shop windows, posters instructing: "Don't shop at the Jews' shops", and with all the employment restrictions, they left Karlsruhe. They moved to Saarbrücken in 1934, just before the province of Sarre was reintegrated into Germany in January 1935. The Sarre had been under a League of Nations Mandate (the region had been divided between Germany and France, somewhat like Alsace). It had been German before the First World War, which is why my grandfather had fought as a German against the French army.

I knew no other member of my grandfather's family. My grandparents were first cousins: my grandmother's father, Jacob Bock, was the brother of my grandfather's mother, Rosalie Bock. They met at a family wedding in Fürth. My grandmother considered this a shame and never wanted to talk about it! My great-grandfather, Jacob Bock was born on November 10, 1839 in Bechhofen in Bavaria. He was not devout, marrying Elisabeth Wittman a Lutheran, born in the neighboring village of Krottenbach on February 3, 1859. They had 13 children.

Rosalie Bock, my great grandaunt and great grandmother married Moses Aron, who was born on 21 June 1822 in Homburg. Their eldest son, my grandfather Isidor Aron, was born in this town on 2 January 1875.

My grandmother, Bertha Bock, the daughter of Jacob, was born on 12 January 1880 in Munich, where the young Bock family had settled. They then settled in Fürth, a town not far from Nuremberg. My great grandfather was a hops trader in this land of beer! It was in Furth that their children grew up. They went to school, learnt a trade, foreign languages and music. My grandmother chose to learn to play the zither, which was fashionable at the time. It was a very united family.

My grandparents set up home in Nuremberg when they married. They had a son Walter, born in 1902, then my mother Alice, born on 30 June 1903. Uncle Paul was born on 30 April 1906. Soon after this date two commercial possibilities became available to my grandfather: one was in Karlsruhe and the other in Basel in Switzerland. He chose Karlsruhe. Subsequent events showed that he made the wrong choice.

In Karlsruhe the couple found an apartment at 55 Kaiserstrasse, a very fine building opposite the Polytechnic College. Their last son, my uncle Martin, was born there in 1907. They lived in Karlsruhe until 1934. My grandfather's business flourished. His firm, J. Aron, imported world famous woolen fabrics from Great Britain, such as Harris tweeds.

My grandfather was religious, the only one in the family. He considered himself to be a good German, of Jewish faith. He became an important man within the community of Karlsruhe; he was very tolerant of others, both Jews and non-Jews. But his religiousness was a disaster for my mother and indirectly led to her death.

My grandmother Bertha followed her husband in practicing the rules of the Jewish faith. Her cooking was Kosher, that is to say, organized according to the rules of Jewish orthodoxy. This even though she had not really had a religious upbringing. My great grandmother had retained her Protestant tradition and it was said for example, that she liked to sing Protestant hymns to her children.

On 11 June 1915, tragedy struck the family: the drowning of their son Walter in a swimming pool at the age of 13. He was preparing to jump from the high diving board when another boy pushed him, and he suffered a cardiac arrest. My grandmother talked to me about it from time to time, and I often think of my grandfather, who had gone with his son that day, and had to break the news to his wife.

Apart from this tragedy, the family was happy in Karlsruhe. The other three children studied in technical or commercial high schools. In addition, my mother studied the piano for many years and became an excellent pianist. My uncles, Paul and Martin liked walking, skiing and tennis. They belonged to sports clubs, as was the custom at the beginning of the 20th century. From what my grandmother said, they started violin lessons, but abandoned them quickly, preferring athletic activities.

My mother was a member of the artistic community of Karlsruhe and Munich. In Karlsruhe, the family knew the painter August Rumm, who painted a series of country scenes, views of around his village, Grötzingen. He also painted a marvelous portrait of my mother in 1929. This large picture depicts her seated, studying sheet music, framed in her favorite colors. This painting as well as some others survived WW2. Her portrait has surrounded me by her presence all my life.

My mother played the piano for friends and family. This was how she met an architect, Mr. Edmond Liebisch, in 1924 or 25. They fell in love and became unofficially engaged. To her great regret and distress, when my mother told her father, he was opposed to the marriage. Mr. Liebisch was not Jewish. The only daughter of a prominent member of the Jewish community could not marry a Protestant! Did my mother ever recover from this sorrow?

Some years later she met my father, Kurt Deichmann, at her father's business, where he was employed. It is difficult to imagine two more dissimilar people. When my mother's brothers asked her why she was marrying him, she apparently replied, "at 29 years old, whom else can I expect?" It was a time when it was shameful to be an "old maid". It was different for my uncles, who were some years younger than my mother; they married at a more "ripe" age, in his forties for uncle Martin in London, and in his fifties for uncle Paul in New York. No doubt the war played a part, but male privilege an even greater one!

In my view, and perhaps in others as well, my parents' marriage on 30 July 1931 was a well calculated arrangement. My maternal grandfather appreciated the work of my father, and my paternal grandfather, Ivan Deichmann, was happy to marry his son into a well-established firm with a reputation going back to the beginning of the century.

My parents set up their home in an apartment building on 8b Südenstrasse corner Karlstrasse. I was born there on the night of Friday 18 November 1932, ten weeks before Hitler came to power.

In 1933, from the time of Hitler's accession to power, restrictions on movement and the persecution of Jews began. My grandfather's business was ransacked. He could no longer work. At the age of 58 he decided to return to the Saarland (Sarre) with his wife. The Sarre was still under the League of Nations Mandate. After a few months in Colmar, France, they moved to Saarbrücken in 1934.

No member of the four branches of my family was Zionist and none went to live in Israel.

La Destruction des juifs d'Europe I, Raul Hilberg, Gallimard, 1985.
Juden in Homburg, Dieter Blinn, Ermer, 1993.

Marion DEICHMANN – Family Tree

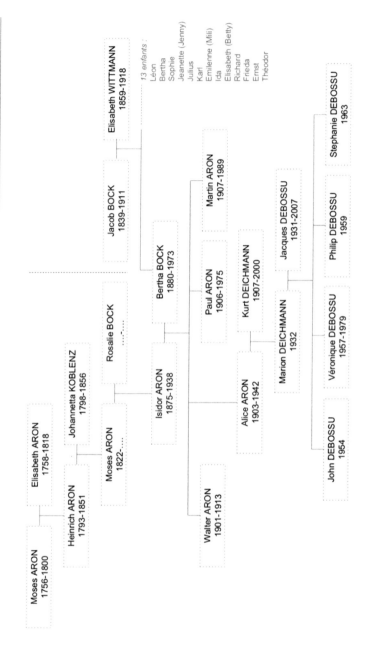

IV - Early childhood in Germany (1932 -1934)

I have no conscious memories of the first months of my life. But I was told of one thing in particular. A photo was taken of me on a family visit to Nuremberg in 1933. I was eleven months old. The photographer took several shots, one of which was quite original for the time: I was sucking my thumb. She decided to put the photo in her shop window. Not a good idea, as a Nazi passing the window thought that I looked Jewish and had the photo removed!

This was a somber forewarning of the way in which a whole people would be overwhelmed by racist madness.

I lived about eighteen months in Karlsruhe, but as my father couldn't find work, my parents and I left Germany in the spring of 1934 and went to live in Luxembourg. However, we frequently went back to Germany to visit my mother's parents.

Visits with my grandparents in Saarbrücken (1934 – 1938)

On their arrival in Saarbrücken my grandparents had rented a large, very comfortable apartment on 11 Karcherstrasse. It became, for a while, the meeting place for family reunions.

I loved my maternal grandparents very much, and I believe these feelings were reciprocated. Until his premature death when I was five, my grandfather, Isidor, was the best of grandfathers. He was more lighthearted than my grandmother, who was no doubt weighed down by worry. She had always been a second mother to me, particularly after my mother's death. Although there were never any visits from the Aron family at my grandparents' home, there were always plenty from my grandmother's brothers and sisters. My grandfather had married the whole Bock "*clan*"

My grandparents were always ready to play with me. Being an only child and their only grandchild - I always lived in a world of adults, and they became my playmates. Sometimes, when my grandfather and I were out for a walk, we would pass by the toyshop and I could pick out a toy I liked. If it wasn't too expensive it was given to me the next time I visited. These precious toys disappeared gradually over the period of our persecutions, but I still have the memory of the pleasure they gave me. Nuremberg at that time was known as the world capital of toys...

In the large spaces of my grandparents' apartment there were many possibilities for me to create a small world of my own. The front door opened into a long hall from which led a wide corridor giving access to all the rooms. Opposite were a large living room, the dining room, and a small salon with a sliding door. My mother's two brothers and in particular my grandmother's sisters and niece often visited and the small salon could be turned into a temporary bedroom. This is where I slept with my mother. In addition there were three bedrooms including my grandparents bedroom with its large white marble bathroom. This large bedroom also became an important place for me, as my grandfather often rested there when he was suffering from cancer.

In the living room there was an "*erker*", a projection out of the façade, a kind of bay window. You had to climb two steps to get to it. Grandmother usually used it for her sewing and other needlework, but it became "*my house*" when I was there, and she stayed "*down*" in the small salon. There were enormous tapestries representing the four seasons. I would have preferred them to be of brighter colors! I was very attracted to my grandfather's large library. Not because of the books – they had no pictures – but because of the little folding glass doors that I played with. I drew in drawing books with fat yellow pencils, survivors of the business in Karlsruhe.

Daily life was well organized in my grandparents' household. Monday was washing day with a meal of sausages and lentils. There was market day, the day the seamstress came, an evening of theatre or hosting a dinner, and obviously the eve and the day of Shabbat, a time of prayer, and Sunday of outings. Because of the laws against Jews, my grandparents were to dismiss their housekeeper, as it was now forbidden for Jews to employ "*Aryans*". So I helped my grandmother do the cooking. Kosher cooking is complicated. Everything is done twice. It is crucial not to mix dairy products with meat products. But once I made a mistake: I wrongly used a knife. So I had to put it in a pot full of garden soil for several days to decontaminate it! It was also customary to invite a poor man to come and eat in the well-lit kitchen; he would come and then leave.

Grandmother kept all the family heirlooms in one room, all her treasures, including the zither. I would try to pluck the metal strings to get some sound from it. But alas, it is a very difficult instrument to play. My uncles had severely damaged it, according to my grandmother! My mother was the only accomplished musician in her family but the others were all avid music lovers. As for my grandfather, I was never sure if he really appreciated music or whether he just accompanied his wife. He sang very off-key, that I do remember.

One day, when I was around four years old, my grandfather took me to see the town's circus. Once we had found our seats, as I was watching the animals and the animal tamer's whip, I didn't want to stay: I asked my grandfather to leave. I think he was very disappointed. After this experience I have never again been to a circus!

My parents separated when I was four years old. My father became increasingly absent, and my grandfather became my father figure from then on. Between 1934 and

1938 we travelled frequently from Luxembourg to Saarbrucken.

The journeys by train from the city of Luxembourg, where we had lived since 1938, to Saarbrucken became more and more dangerous. Taking the train exposed a person to frequent police checks. One such trip to Germany was particularly so. I was a very sociable child and was in the habit of talking to strangers. Knowing no better, I replied to the question of one of the guards on the train, when he asked if we had anything to declare. I revealed that I had my doll in my little suitcase together with a packet of coffee. My poor mother went pale, most likely because there were restrictions on the import of certain goods. Fortunately, the guard left it at that. German Jews had become stateless and my parents had not been able to obtain residents permit for Luxembourg, so we were living there clandestinely. Then, as in other moments, we had needed much luck to escape the manhunts. I would often remind myself of this ...

I also remember that before Christmas, on 6 December Saint Nicolas always visited the northern European towns. He gathered up a procession that wound its way through the streets of the town, followed by a character called the "*Père Fouettard*" who would punish children who had not been good. I had a bad conscience, having disobeyed my mother, so I was a little bit afraid. On one Saint Nicolas' eve, 6 December 1937, while visiting my very sick grandfather, he called for me to sleep beside him. He had previously asked my grandmother to bring him his saber from the First World War to protect me, and had placed it next to him. Like the majority of Germans, my grandparents slept in single beds and I was afraid that the saber would fall between the two beds! But I soon fell asleep in my grandmother's bed with the saber between grandfather and me.

My beloved grandfather, "*Opa*", died on 2 March 1938. He was 63 and I was 5. I knew that something very important had just happened, but I didn't fully understand its meaning. I knew grandfather had gone, but I had no notion of this "*other place*". Many grownups were coming and going in the apartment. Grandmother or mother opened the front door; I would go out onto the landing and straddle the banister, letting myself slide gently down to the first turn in the stairs. My mother would come looking for me and would scold me gently. I had always been a very active child.

So as not to risk crossing the border one more time, my mother and I stayed in Saarbrucken with my grandmother until the end of April, never to return again to Germany. During that time, in spite of the restrictions imposed through the race laws, some members of my grandmother's family came together in mutual support, particularly my great-aunt Ida.

When grandmother left Saarbrucken at the end of 1938, she left her furniture in storage. She was forced to pay 10 years in advance. She came to Paris to find her son Paul, travelling with two suitcases containing her clothes. Later the family learned that all of the furniture and possessions stored had been stolen and/or auctioned off in 1939.

V - Luxembourg (1934 -1940)

Along with memories of my grandparents, this is how I remember my daily life of that time. We settled in Luxembourg in March 1934, in the small wine-growing commune of Remich - 10 km from the well-known town of Schengen and 80 km from Saarbrucken. My father still had cousins and friends there, having spent holidays there in his childhood. He himself was born on 23 July 1907 very close by in Algrange, in French Lorraine.

My paternal grandmother was Luxembourgish from birth. She was born on 22 January 1876 in Remich. The town had been a county seat and a commercial crossroad since the Middle Ages. At the beginning of the twentieth century wine growing started to develop and it still exists today. Luxembourg has three cultures. Sometimes French dominates, sometimes German, always with distinctive features of its own. There are three official languages: Luxembourgish, German and French. Apart from German that we spoke at home, I only spoke Luxembourgish.

My parents found a house right at the end of one of the main roads of Remich, at 54 rue Macher. This road is still bordered on one side by the Moselle and on the other by vineyards. Our garden went right up to the vines. We crossed the road and a meadow to go swimming. It felt so good there! The house was not big but was large enough for our family and for all the visitors, members of my mother's family, who at the beginning often came to visit us.

When we moved to Luxembourg the race laws had not yet been promulgated. We still had German nationality and passports bearing no distinctive marks. Thus my parents were able to move and take all their possessions with them.

The house was furnished like the apartment in Karlsruhe. My bed was in my parents' bedroom. There was a lounge, two guest bedrooms with bathroom, the kitchen, and a large dining room. The table and chairs were in the center, towards the window. The sideboard was on one side and beyond that, in the corner, was a glass-fronted cupboard containing all my mother's treasures – miniatures and porcelain statuettes and other objects dear to her. They fascinated me and I spent long moments admiring them. The decoration of this room also impressed me enormously, painted in my mother's favorite colors. She liked all the shades of brown, russet and pink. Her piano dominated the room, and it was here that we spent most of our time. We knitted and sewed. When I was bored I upended the lacquered wooden chairs. I have no recollection of a radio or gramophone. All my early childhood is soothed by the music of my mother's piano. I never recovered any of her sheet music, but the sweetness of the melodies makes me think she played the music of Schubert. Her cousin Elisabeth told me much later that she was very fond of the music of Debussy. I didn't spend much time in the living room. My mother's portrait lit it up. She was the only member of the close family to have had her portrait painted. It survived the subsequent tragedy.

The house also had a huge attic. Just where the two chimneys emerged there was a "*smoking cupboard*" a little cupboard where sausages and meat would be hung to dry. I liked to go up there with my mother when she hung out the washing.

I was just two years old when I had whooping cough; it was the only childhood illness I caught. One of my first memories was sucking my thumb, a habit that my mother wanted me to give up. As I was coughing a lot, she gave me a pacifier dipped in honey. However, once I'd swallowed the honey I started to cry again, wanting to suck my bandage-wrapped thumb. She very quickly gave in!

I was a very inquisitive child. The solitude of my isolation made me want to discover my surroundings. A female cat had had a litter of kittens and they became my dolls. I dressed them up, unintentionally making them suffer. I also played with insects. I didn't understand why my mother was scared of spiders and mice: I considered all these creatures to be my friends!

Then there were the memories of my father which were much less happy. My parents' relationship was worsening as each day passed. They had not yet learned to live as a couple, when they found themselves living as three, in circumstances that were getting worse and worse with time. The race laws were passed and implemented: we were refugees from Germany and we had lost our nationality, our status, and our identity. About 3000 Jews were in the same situation in Luxembourg. My father tried very hard to look for work in the commercial sector, but didn't find any. He wrote letters not only to within Luxembourg but also to France and to England. All the replies were negative even his application to join the Foreign Legion. He ended up taking work as a farm hand. Their savings were disappearing at a very fast rate. My father often stayed away from home, and when he came back he was unpleasant to us.

I wanted a big brother. As a stork brought these, I tried to tame it with my most precious possession: chocolate, which I placed on the window ledge. That didn't work and I quickly realized why. I saw my father eat the chocolate. This was a huge disappointment.

To add to our woes, in 1936-37 the Moselle burst its banks; our basement was flooded. That year I attended the kindergarten in the center of the village. Since the roads were under water, we went in a rowing boat. I found myself in the boat with my father. I undoubtedly moved around a lot and he slapped me and told me to stay still. I was stunned. I had been slapped three times in my life. This was the first and the last from my father. The following year, in 1938, my parents separated *"officially"* and I didn't see my father until 44 years later. I asked him then: why did you slap me? He replied that he didn't know how to swim and was afraid the boat would capsize!

We had many visitors up until July 1938, and still visited Germany until April of that same year. In spite of the breakup of my parents' marriage, my mother had good relations with my father's elder brother, Erich. He was a friendly and good man and had lived for a long time in Brazil, since well before the advent of the Nazis. He visited us several times in Remich. He did not approve at all of my father's lifestyle before leaving for Brazil. Later, my mother wrote to her brother-in-law several times to ask for his help to immigrate to Brazil. Distressing letters, which my aunt and my cousins gave me when my father died. But it had been to late. The Jews who had stayed in Europe were now caught in a trap.

The visits were principally from my mother's family, from my grandparents, *"Oma"* and *"Opa"*, my uncles, my great-aunts and cousins of my mother, and they filled me with joy. I would like to draw a few portraits, as most of the thirteen children of my great grandparents did not have any children. Of the seven daughters, only two married Jews, one of which, my grandmother, had four children. Of the five others only one had three children. The daughters were all Christians. The six sons were evenly divided between Christians/without religion and Jews. Only one had a child, a daughter Erika, who was just two years older than me.

There was aunt Ida, unmarried, a practicing Protestant. She was my mother's favorite aunt, and was fifteen years older than her. She was born in Furth on 6 September 1888. She was the *"intellectual"* of the brothers and sisters, lived in Munich and my mother often visited her there. She had obtained the *"Abitur"* – German baccalaureate-which in those days and in a family of 13 brothers and sisters was quite an achievement! My first clear memory of aunt Ida dates back to 1938, on 16 April; it was Easter, in Saarbrucken, a little after the death of my grandfather. We went on a walk together. She intimidated me. It was very formal and I had to be well behaved! She was not used to children. She also came to visit us in Remich. After the war, in New York, she became my favorite of the few surviving aunts.

From August 1938 onwards it became more difficult to travel outside of Germany. For on all passports the first name had to be preceded or followed by the name "*Sara*" for women and "Israel" for men. Also, on 5 October of that year, at the request of the Swiss authorities, the German authorities stamped our passports with a capital J in red or black ink. This enabled them to more easily identify German Jews who presented themselves at the border.

Aunt Ida stayed in Germany until 9 September 1940. On that date she went to Berlin and travelled, by train, across Russia and Manchuria to arrive in Shanghai on 18 September. From Shanghai she took a boat to Cuba, and then another to New York, in 1941! She was there to greet us when we disembarked in 1947. She was an important part of my adolescence. I loved her very much, in spite of her strictness. Memories of her have stayed with me all my life, right up to her death in New York in November 1970, just after I had visited her for the last time. She suffered from Parkinson's disease.

Elisabeth also visited us. I still visit her now, in Furth or in Vienna at her son's house. Elizabeth was born on 8 April 1920. She is my mother's cousin and is 17 years younger than her. She is the youngest daughter of Emilie, one of my grandmother's younger sisters, and the elder of my grandparents' two nieces and, in her own opinion, very spoiled by them. She often came to see us after I was born and often babysat me. I called her "Lela".

Erika was my mother's other cousin. She was born on 3 September 1930 and was thus two years older than me. My mother was often in Munich and enjoyed the company of her uncle Ernst and his wife Hilde, Erika's parents. We continued to visit them up until 1938. Erika lived with her parents in a very fine house. I have only one clear memory: we were playing with dolls, both of us sitting on the stairs. My beautiful cousin Erika with blond hair and blue eyes was deported after a major roundup in Munich and assassinated by the Nazis, with her parents and two aunts, Jenny and Sophie. They were killed by firing squad near Kaunas, Lithuania 25 November 1941 with over 1,000 other Jews on that particular day. This was what was called the Holocaust (Shoah) by firing squad".

My great-aunt Jenny came once to Remich. She was the tallest of the Bock girls and the 4th of the 13 Bock children. She had married a certain Midas, whom I never met. He was a man of fortune, famous for his library that was enormous. Aunt Jenny worked as a volunteer nurse during the war before being assassinated.

My uncles Paul and Martin came when they could. They kept in close touch with my mother by letter. Uncle Martin worked in London before the war: obviously he stayed there. He was nevertheless interned for a short period on the Isle of Man, because he was a German – the enemy! It was uncle Paul who was very involved in the survival of my grandmother, my mother and myself. It was to him that my grandmother came on the death of her husband. It was also to his home that my mother and I went after the invasion of Luxembourg and France by the Germans. He was my father figure during my adolescence.

Remich was the place where I lived happily with my mother, my cats, and my few garden flowers. It was in Remich that I had my first toothache. Not surprising, since I loved sweet things and chocolate. My mother dragged me across the village. I cried, I screamed: I didn't want to go to the dentist. Of course there were no anesthetics then.

We stopped going to Germany. On 22 July 1939 every Jew had to get a "Kennkarte", an identity card with a large J printed on the cover, as well as another that took up around one third of the following page. A few weeks earlier the Evian conference had been held. It was a meeting of delegates from 32 countries to discuss the situation of Jewish refugees in Europe. They created the International Refugee Committee (IRC). This committee had little power and fewer resources, and it was never very active. None of the 32 countries, although sympathizing with the plight of the refugees, allowed any in. Certain countries such as Cuba allowed a very small number to transit. Only the Dominican Republic agreed to accept a large number.

Then there was Cristal Night, in Germany, on 9 – 10 November. On this night the Nazis burned and destroyed synagogues and everything that belonged to the Jews. There were also police raids. My paternal grandfather was interned in the Buchenwald concentration camp on 11 November 1938. My uncle Erich, his son, managed to have him released and transferred to Hanover 11 days later, through the intervention of the Brazilian Consul. My paternal grandparents received their emigration visas and left for Brazil before the end of that year. This was possibly thanks to Mrs Aracy de Carvalho, a great Brazilian resistance worker and head of the "passport" section in Hamburg.

My father left Luxembourg in October 1938 and set sail from Antwerp in Belgium to Rio de Janeiro on 26 January 1939. My mother, from whom he was separated, didn't want to go with him. She didn't want to follow him without members of her own family. Not realizing the danger of staying behind, she didn't want to be in any way indebted to my father or her former in-laws, who she thought were hostile to her. Only uncle Erich had invited her to follow them.

So we had to leave Remich for the last time and live in an apartment in Luxembourg City. It was at 22 avenue de la

Liberté, on a broad avenue in a modern, commercial district. Times became very difficult for my mother. Life had become serious and sad, and I felt it. I went to school there from 1938 to 1940, the kindergarten class and first year of primary school. In spite of everything they were happy times for the young child I was. I often played dolls with my friend Jacqueline. But I was more of a tomboy and played happily with the boys at playtime. I borrowed my mother's bicycle one day in 1939 and found myself cycling downhill. My hands were too small for the adult bike and I didn't grab the breaks in time. I did a somersault, went under a fence and ended up in a field full of horses. They came to get a closer look and scared me half to death. I retrieved the bike and went home sheepishly. I had damaged the handlebars of my mother's bike and it bothered me to have given her something further to worry about.

My first experience of death came with the death of the mother of one of my school friends. Before the burial we had to gather in front of her coffin that was in her home. The whole class went up the stairs in single file and went into the bedroom. Under the cover of glass this woman was the incarnation of Sleeping Beauty: dressed in white, lying on white satin, very beautiful and apparently sleeping… Death was not horrible at all; I was six years old and was not afraid.

I celebrated my last Christmas combined with Hanukkah in Luxembourg City. My mother made a spray of branches, which she placed on the landing and decorated. That year, on 6 December I also went to see the great Saint Nicolas procession followed by Père Fouettard.

There was a fair in the spring of 1939 that we went to, my mother and I. Two things happened. One was happy since I won a doll that turned its head from left to right as it walked. The other was worrying: a gypsy came up to my mother and took her hand to tell her fortune. She said several things and then added that she would live a "passage through fire". She stopped there. My mother was alarmed by this apocalyptic vision and didn't move for several moments. I had of course heard the prediction but couldn't understand it. In fact I don't know if my mother could take it in. One can't really imagine hell. Of course the Dachau, Buchenwald and other concentration camps already existed and the gypsy, a clever analyst of human nature guessed my mother's origins. Nevertheless, the gas chambers did not yet exist at that time. We returned home in a sad mood.

My mother knew the fate of the Jews in Germany. She tried to immigrate to Brazil with aunt Ida and I. In a heartrending letter dated 15 January 1939, my mother asked her brother-in-law to help her to leave for Rio. She spoke highly of my aunt's talents, emphasizing that she was highly qualified in foreign languages – in addition to German she could write and speak English, French and Italian. But emigration to Brazil was no longer possible.

In March Germany began invading the countries of Eastern Europe and broke all existing agreements. Our situation became more precarious. Since she couldn't find work, my mother took in a second boarder for one of the bedrooms of the apartment. She contacted her brothers with a view to joining them. Early in February we celebrated "Chandeleur" based on a Christian holyday. In France it is customary to eat crepes. In Luxembourg as children we walked in the streets with paper lanterns, visiting the grocery stores asking for food. A few doors down from our house was a dairy. I particularly liked the Kochkäse, the Luxembourgish soft cooked cheese, and I was given a spoonful.

The months went past. We no longer had visitors. War was declared on 3 September 1939. The following week, on 11 September 1939, my mother wrote a letter to her brother in London in which she explained that one of the boarders had left. She began to sell the living room furniture, the dining room furniture, some fine china, some works of art and of course, the piano. The two of us occupied one bedroom and the kitchen. She read in a newspaper that the English thought the war would last at least three years. She couldn't believe it. 11 September 1939 was also the first day of second grade. I loved school. The little only child who was normally surrounded by adults, discovered children of her own age and enjoyed a more cheerful atmosphere.

My mother was in constant contact with her brothers and received news from Paris and London. In Paris, grandmother was unwell in the latter part of the winter of 1939-1940. My mother sent another letter to Martin dated 18 March 1940 in which she said that she had received a letter from the Ministry asking her to leave Luxembourg within two months: her visa was not renewed. Again my mother asked her two brothers to help her to leave. On 10 May 1940 German troops invaded neutral Luxembourg. My school was divided in two. We shared the building and the schoolyard with the German troops. One day, in the schoolyard, in full view of the children, the soldiers caught a pig. It was killed with an axe and cut into pieces. I was nauseous and felt sick. This barbaric act was an indication of what was to follow. Anti-Semitism could be seen in people's eyes/looks. Was it pure coincidence that when I went to buy candies, the shopkeeper put them in a bag with ground pepper at the bottom. At any rate, I had a sore throat and sneezed for quite a while. We stayed nonetheless until September 1940.

The 1935 Nuremberg race laws were introduced to Luxembourg on 5 September 1940. However, the exclusion from private and public working places as well as denunciation were practiced well before that date. Now this became openly approved and encouraged.

As recently as 2013, a historian and professor from the University of Luxembourg, Denis Scuto, discovered in the Luxembourg national archives a list of 280 primary school children dated September 1940. The teachers drew up this list on the request of the school superintendent, a Nazi collaborator. It was entitled "Teachers and students of non-Aryan origin"

It was a great choc for me to find my name on the list as well as that of my young friend, Jacqueline. It was then easy to track down these children and their family for future deportation to Hitler's death camps. This was, unfortunately, the fate of Jacqueline who was deported and assassinated in Auschwitz in 1943.

The expulsion order for the Jews of Luxembourg was issued on 12 September 1940. My mother found a way out. I don't know how. Two wooden cases containing the possessions that she wanted to keep were entrusted to a friend, Madame Didong. They contained the oil paintings, including my mother's portrait, watercolors, and a selection of china and linens.

On a fine day at the end of summer, on the day that the head of the Gestapo gave the ultimatum to Jews to leave the country, we passed into Belgium, on our way to France. We had two large suitcases containing our clothes, a few valuable items, two of my dolls and a few children's books in German.

The train took us to Brussels where we stayed the night in a good hotel. Unfortunately many German soldiers were staying there. When evening came I was very hungry but my mother didn't want to run the risk of going down to the dining room. Our stay there was therefore short and unpleasant. The following morning, very early, we left the hotel with our suitcases. But with no visas!

A canvas-covered truck was waiting for us in a side street. We climbed aboard, beside the driver, which I thought was fun. To pass the Belgium-France border we had to hide between crates, our suitcases and under coarse sacks. The truck was bumping along the main road that went from Belgium into France, when all of a sudden the driver braked and stopped. My heart did a flip and no doubt my mother's too. I instinctively understood the danger. I heard the sound of boots on the asphalt. Then voices. They were checking the driver's papers and came round and lifted the canvas slightly. We stopped breathing. We were hunted animals.

Finally, after several minutes that lasted centuries, the motor started up again. We were in France, which, like Luxembourg, had been invaded by enemy troops since June 1940, but was divided into two zones. One was occupied and governed by the Nazis. The other, the free zone, was led by the Vichy government and Marshall Petain, Nazi collaborators.

We entered the occupied zone.

VI - France, September 1940

Yes, we were in France. Thousands of French people had been thrown onto the roads. We arrived after that exodus. I was not yet eight years old, and I spoke no French or very little. Luxembourgish was unknown outside the borders of the country, and German was a banned language, forbidden and disgraced - except for collaborators, Petainists, anti-Semites and other admirers of the Nazis.

But I was with my mother and my world was complete. With her I felt secure and reassured. Obviously I didn't understand her fears and anxieties... I didn't ask her why we had fled. I didn't fully realize that we were being hunted and in danger of death. Probably my mother herself didn't fully realize the horror, even though rumors had started early on about the internment camps and the work camps: "Arbeit macht frei", "Work makes you free". Before being put up at the entrance to the Auschwitz camp, this sentence was written on the frame of the entrance gate to the Dachau internment camp, which all German Jews knew of well before the war.

My first experience in France was in the café of a railway station, a little while after crossing the border. It was a sunny terrace. The contrast was welcome after being hidden under a canvas in a truck for a long time. We were sitting at a table near a low stonewall. A couple occupied the only other table near ours. They talked to me. I smiled at them and looked at my mother. She spoke French well, but with a strong German accent. She translated their words for me and I was able to reply "yes and thank you very much" in French. I don't think I understood what it was all about and I had a strong feeling of inadequacy.

VII - Paris from 1940 to July 1942

Arrival (1940 – 1941)

We came to France because that is where uncle Paul had lived and worked since before the war. He arrived at the beginning of the thirties to learn the language, a student living in rue Royer-Collard, in Paris. He got to like it, and stayed. He worked for an aluminum company as an overseas representative. After the death of my grandfather, grandmother had joined him and lived with him in Paris, but she soon found herself living alone again. In fact, when we arrived Paul was gone. Soon after the declaration of war, in September 1939, he was interned as a foreigner in one of those internment camps, the "Colombes Stadium", then sent as a "forced laborer" in one of the companies for foreign workers (Compagnie de Travailleurs Etrangers) stationed at that time in Villeurbon, in Lot et Cher.

We arrived in Paris without my having really noticed how we crossed France. In Paris we took the metro to get to the apartment at 12 rue Gustave Lebon in the 14th arrondissement, where grandmother was living. Soon after our arrival and the previous departure of uncle Paul we had to leave the apartment; it had been rented by uncle Paul in his own name, and in his absence, by two women and a child, defenseless, with no income, with no residence papers, no official status, struggling to find enough food – we couldn't stay there.

Paul was 33 years old at the defeat of France on 10 July 1940. He tried to reach England. At St Nazaire a small group of Legionnaires tried to embark on a small British ship, but because they were foreigners the English threw them off. My uncle then went to the southwest "Free zone", trying to reach the Spanish border. He was arrested twice in round ups in Toulouse. He told me later how he escaped.

French policemen had arrested him. The weather was very hot. He suggested going for a beer in a café that he knew of. He knew there were two entrances to the café. He sat down with them, and then suddenly mentioned that he had to go to the toilet. The policemen let him go. Paul escaped through the back door and managed to hide in a farm, where he was then taken on as a farm worker - He stayed with this farmer for several months.

Paul wanted to look up a pre-war friend, Hans Isenberg, who had joined the Foreign Legion and was now hiding in Bagneres de Bigorre. But he was arrested again at an identity check and sent to another internment camp not only for Jews but also anti-Franco Spaniards, gypsies, and traffickers and other criminals: the Récébédou internment camp near Toulouse. There were many camps in this region[1]. Surprisingly for a non-practicing Jew, in spite of gnawing hunger, he couldn't bring himself to eat ham. Or rats....

On August 17, 1942 uncle Paul wrote very moving words on a card addressed to grandmother. Shortly thereafter that camp was included in Hitler's final solution and three convoys of prisoners were sent to the deaths camps in Eastern Europe via Drancy near Paris. The activities of camp Recebedou were stopped through the intervention of Toulouse's Archbishop Salieges in September 1942

To survive he once again showed amazing initiative. One evening, on his own, between two watchtowers' light beams, he crawled on his stomach under the barbed wire. He knew that if he stayed he would be deported to one of the concentration camps in Poland. He escaped and hid in Bagnères de Bigorre. I wrote two postcards to him there, one from my mother and one from my grandmother, to "Paul Aron, poste restante - general delivery, Bagneres de

---

[1] Les Juifs pendant l'occupation, André Kaspi, Seuil, 1991 et 1997

Bigorre, Upper Pyrenees". They were special postcards "reserved exclusively for family correspondence". They were censured.

The writing was somewhat coded, for though I wrote and signed them, my mother dictated them, to tell him that we were well and all three of us still alive. I didn't see my uncle Paul until five years later in December 1944, when I returned to Paris from Normandy.

Back to 1940.

We had to leave the apartment. Mother and grandmother had found a much more affordable studio in the working class district of Le Marais at 12 rue Caffarelli, Paris 3eme. We lived in this furnished studio until July 1942.

It was very different from the social surroundings that I had known up until then. It had cold running water, a gas heater, a toilet on the outside corridor, and to take a bath or a shower we had to go to the public baths. In spite of it being so small, there was a screen in front of a washbasin, and my mother, who had very strict personal hygiene, washed her whole body every morning in cold water. And she encouraged me to do the same. I must admit that I cheated! After washing, whenever possible, my mother drank a large glass of water with lemon when available. This was so different to the grand marble bathroom of my grandparents' home, but we had to adapt. What was important for me was to be close to my mother and my grandmother. The place and the environment were not important at all. Looking back, I feel that for a little girl of eight years old, what was important was the unconditional love that my mother and grandmother gave me. I felt secure, in spite of the hostile and unfamiliar world that surrounded me.

Throughout 1940-41 we adapted to our new situation with its new restrictions. The race laws against the Jews were soon to be promulgated. We were very much alone; my grandmother had been in Paris since 1939 and knew very few people. Since her French was poor, her few friends were mainly other German Jews. My mother and I knew no one. In the neighborhood where we lived, Yiddish – which we didn't speak – was the second language spoken, after French. My mother spoke and wrote, with mistakes, the French she had learned in high school.

We still had rare exchanges with those of our family who had remained in Germany – those whom the race laws classified as "non-Jews" – Protestants in their case (Evangelisch in German).

In July 1941 we had a visit from Hilde, a friend of my cousin Elisabeth who was in Paris with the Wehrmacht. Hilde, who must have been on leave, was not in uniform. She brought me a few things including a gift from our cousin.

It was a little round watch with a black leather bracelet. It was such a joy for me in that time of hardship! My mother and grandmother were touched by the gesture, since it was dangerous for this friend to associate with Jews. The watch, the first I had owned, got lost during my wanderings, but I remember it with fondness. I was proud to be a big girl, at nine.

My mother and I explored Paris on the metro. She especially liked the above ground lines, Nation – Porte Dauphine, Place d'Italie – Etoile and Place d'Italie – Gare du Nord. We walked around for hours at a time, often on Sundays. The mass arrests hadn't started; the Star of David wasn't worn.

We also walked along the Rue de Rivoli, window-shopping. My mother was very shortsighted, but since she didn't like to be seen wearing glasses, she was always asking me the price of skirts and clothing on display. I was also the eyes of my grandmother, who suffered from cataract.

My grandmother was elegant and refined, but very Bavarian. She often came to pick me up from school. Once we were sitting outside on the Place de la Republique; it was very hot. At a little round table on the café terrace I was given lemonade, and there was my grandmother, elegant as usual: hat and lace gloves, light summer dress and little handbag. At the time of day when every grandmother in the world would be drinking tea, my grandmother ordered a beer. I was embarrassed.

She was a lady, always elegant, no Bavarian bumpkin. But she was also the child of a hop dealer, born to the world of beer. I associated that with "non-French", with being German, perhaps a little vulgar and certainly strange – while I wanted to go unnoticed. It seemed to me that by drinking beer there, grandmother was revealing her identity, which I always tried to conceal, by speaking French and not making waves.

Early in 1941, I lost my baby teeth and my adult teeth grew in. My two front teeth were side by side, but one was growing outward and the other inward. When I closed my mouth, the lower jaw was stuck between those two teeth. My mother consulted a German dentist, an expert in this technique, whose practice was on Avenue Kleber or Avenue Foch, near the Arc de Triomphe.

In those days there were no dental braces, since the technique was in its infancy. Having tried the technique on a dog's teeth, he made a brace that he set on my lower incisors. It was like a mountain of resin in my mouth that I had to bite on to push the wayward tooth in the right direction, aligning it with the other. That was in summer 1941. Going to the dentist, I remember feeling uneasy because he was German. I don't know whether he was Jewish, but I think not. I was supposed to go back for a check-up. After paying the bill, my mother decided not to go back.

All that summer I heard rumors. My mother never spoke to me explicitly of the danger. It was something I sensed in conversations between her and grandmother.

In 1941 my mother wanted to go to the "Victoire" synagogue for Yom Kippur. It was a day she always observed. We were in the street and I was dawdling behind her. She said, "Come on Marion!" A woman stopped and said "You call her by her surname?"

Perhaps the woman was thinking of Paul Marion, a populist and ferocious anti-Semite who was Petain's[2] secretary-general for information and propaganda at the time. It is also true that Marion, as a first name, was not in fashion at the time in France. With that mediaeval name, my mother had unwittingly given me an international name that has been very convenient.

As soon as we moved to Rue Caffarelli my mother enrolled me in the Beranger public primary school for the 1940-41 school year. It was the local school for girls. I had previously been to school in Luxembourg, where my first two years were in German, which was the language I read and wrote at the time. Still, Luxembourg had a mixed culture with a French-speaking history, and so I understood a little French. At the French school I tried as hard as I could to conceal the weakness of my French, and not to show that I did not always understand the teacher's instructions.

My first dictation went badly. The teacher read the entire text; the students were supposed to listen first then to write when she repeated the text phrase by phrase, with pauses so we could keep up. I hadn't grasped that, and tried to write the entire text out very quickly from memory as soon as she had read it through. When she saw I was writing she came over to me and slapped my face. I felt so humiliated. I didn't know where to look. She was a very pretty young woman whose husband was a prisoner in Germany; she clearly regretted it. Was she anti-Semitic or anti-German? For me, she could have been either. It was hard to be both Jewish and German in that situation. It was a double burden

---

[2] L'Occupation allemande en France, Jean Defrasne, P.U.F., 1985.

throughout the war. In spite of the injustice of it, which I feel to this day, I never held it against her.

In spite of everything, I quickly adapted to French, and at the end of that school year I won the class first prize, a beautiful book of children's stories.

Every morning between 8 and 9 o'clock, grandmother or I went to buy milk, eggs, butter or margarine at the local store on Rue Caffarelli, very near the apartment. We paid with ration coupons.

Grandmother was scandalized at the French women who went shopping with an overcoat thrown over nightgown, dressing gown and slippers, confirming German prejudices about the French: unwashed, messy (and with loose morals). She would say "Wie kann man nur so aus dem Haus gehen?" "How can they go out dressed like that?" In Germany no one, however humble, would leave the house dressed in that way.

In Paris in those days, tradesmen would push carts along the streets. Some collected rabbit pelts, some were rag men, knife-grinders or window pane replacers. They all announced themselves by shouting "Rabbit rabbit rabbit skins!" or « Knife and scissors »

We had a coal fire. Coalmen drove horse-drawn carts with iron-cased wheels. They stopped at the cellar doors. Every house had a cellar whose doors opened directly onto the pavement, so the bags of coal could be emptied in. The war, the deprivation and the worries of my mother and grandmother made me very sensitive. I was very upset when I saw the coalman beating his skinny horse to make it go faster. I think that was the start of my love, compassion and interest in the lives of animals.

There were no secrets in the street. One sunny day, probably a Thursday school off day, I was going out to play in my spring dress; I had just stepped onto the street to cross it when a drunk man literally fell on top of me. He knocked me off balance but held onto me and kissed me on the mouth. The neighbors were outraged. I didn't want trouble, I just wanted to get away, but the customers in the shop nearby, especially the women, who were horrified, came out onto the sidewalk to deal with the drunk. They wanted to call the police. I fled and didn't mention the incident to my mother or grandmother, but the neighbors told them. The police station and the town hall occupied the entire length of the other side of the street. I often heard people screaming in the police station at night but didn't realize what was going on. People were being tortured.

According to historians, in summer 1939 there were approximately 330,000 Jews in France, in a total population[3] of 41,510,000: equivalent to 0.75% of the population, 4% in Paris. Half were Jews of French origin.

We found ourselves in a trap: the 3rd arrondissement, the Marais, had one of the biggest Jewish populations in Paris, whether long established or recent refugees with their accents and their anxieties.

Between 1940 and 1943 the Nazis, with "the consent, the zeal and the support" of the Vichy régime[4], issued decrees, laws and statutes against the Jews. The Vichy Government copied the text of the Nazi race laws promulgated in Germany in 1935[5]. Shortly after our arrival the first anti-Jewish laws appeared. The first edict of 27 September 1940, which came into force on 3 October, was on the status of Jews. All Jews were to report to their local police station with their identity documents. This is how that edict from Germany affected us: it decided who was and who was not Jewish; all Jews were to register with the local authorities, and the declaration of the head of the household counted for the whole family; failure to comply entailed

---

[3] L'Occupation allemande en France, Jean Defrasne, P.U.F., 1985.
[4] Le Calendrier, Serge Klarsfeld, Fils et filles de déportés juifs de France – F.F.D.J.F., 1993.
[5] L'Allemagne nazie et les juifs I, Saul Friedländer, Seuil, 1997.

imprisonment or a fine[6]. Shopkeepers were subject to particular harassment. We all had to register on the "family file" which was kept at the Seine prefecture of police, and in sub-registers[7]. Registration was done in alphabetical order; the letter D was done on 6 October 1940.

In order to legalize our status in France, my mother hardly thought twice about registering whenever it was required, which was whenever a new edict or law on the status of Jews in France was promulgated. This was because we had no status and were totally illegal aliens. Worse: we were Jews and ex-Germans.

In any event, since we lived across the road from the police station my mother didn't believe that she had much of a choice. As head of the family she registered both of us. I do not know whether my grandmother registered or whether her file was lost. A surname such as Aron was rather obvious to the police. She was listed as a beneficiary of ration coupons, so other files on her must have been made.

Many files were destroyed – particularly those of people who returned after deportation. The files of deportees survived, for the most part. At that stage, only Jews serving in the Foreign Legion were not obliged to register; there were 12,000 of them. My father had written to the Legion from Luxembourg asking to enlist, but he was not accepted.

A total of 149,734 Jewish people were registered in the Seine department, 85,664 of them French and 64,070 foreign. Every family member was registered on the family file[8].

Everyone who went to register had to complete a questionnaire that was typed on cards of various colors by

---

[6] Le Calendrier, Serge Klarsfeld, Fils et filles de déportés juifs de France – F.F.D.J.F., 1993. Les Juifs sous l'Occupation, Recueil des textes officiels français et allemands 1940-1944, Fils et filles de déportés juifs de France – F.F.D.J.F., 1982.
[7] Le Fichier, Annette Kahn, Robert Laffont, 1993
[8] Le Fichier, Annette Kahn, Robert Laffont, 1993, p. 25

the officials. For us, the foreigners, adults and children, they were white.

Then came the individual file for the Seine prefecture of police, required by Pucheu, Secretary of State for the Interior, on 29 July 1941. Those files too were white for foreigners. The individual files bore a capital "J" top left, and the file number for the central police register. All the files were then classified by address, nationality and occupation.

The French administration compiled the data and transmitted them to the German authorities. They were an essential tool for the mass arrests and the crimes that followed.

The first mass arrest took place on 14 May 1941. Men between the ages of 16 and 60 of Polish, Czechoslovak and Austrian nationality were called in.

Thanks to the files, sorting was easy: 6,494 convocations were prepared and put in family mailboxes by the police[9]. Many responded, and those 3,747 men were sent to various camps in France. That mass arrest was an introduction and a rehearsal for what followed.

After the arrests of 14 May, the German authorities and the Paris prefecture of police organized a "full-scale mass arrest, only in the 11th arrondissement of Paris"[10]. That mass arrest began on 20 August 1941, but since it did not bring in enough prisoners, it was extended to other districts until 25 August. 4,230 Jewish men were arrested. In addition to the existing internment camps, the camp of Drancy was opened on 20 August 1941.

Paris, race laws and restrictions (1941 and early 1942)

Our family savings were dwindling by the day; for illegal residents, then as now, it was extremely hard to find work.

---

[9] Ibid
[10] La Rafle du Vel d'hiv, Maurice Rajsfus, P.U.F., 2002.

My mother could have taught piano, German, perhaps even child psychology, but she had to take work as a housekeeper. My mother was very unhappy with that Mrs Hermann, a wealthy German Jew who had been in France since before the war. That woman was unkind and seriously humiliated my mother. The road to her house was noted in my mother's little address book; the latter brings back stressful memories.

The lady's address was 7 rond-point du Pont Mirabeau, near the Place Balard metro station. To get there, we had to change at la Motte-Picquet Grenelle and take the Auteuil line to Javel. Since my grandmother's cataracts could not be treated in those days, her sight was very poor. And as a recent immigrant, her French was poor also. Having had some French schooling and since I had good eyesight, I was her guide and interpreter. Since grandmother liked to meet my mother as she finished work, we took the metro there. We both had our yellow star, though we always concealed it with a shawl or a scarf. At Javel the doors opened and we got off the train. When we had gone a little way up the stair I saw a pair of boots at the top. A Nazi in uniform on the landing was checking the commuters' papers. My blood froze. I had the presence of mind to grab grandmother's arm and rush her back to the train we had just left, managing to reopen the doors before departure. We were safe, but I was shaking with fear.

It was at that metro station that I finally understood the danger we were in, with Paris dominated by the Nazis. The city under the race laws was one large trap where random identity checks could happen anywhere, at any time. I was deeply shaken by that escape. At times I still wake up gasping for breath from dreams where those boots are after me.

Other lists and files were drawn up by other ministries, for allowances of food, tobacco, bread and cloth: whatever was rationed during the war. I was growing and I needed clothes; the textile rations were not enough. My mother was always lengthening dresses and skirts, but that couldn't go on indefinitely. So she added borders to them. In order to keep summer sandals in use for as long as possible she cut the straps at the front, which meant my toes stuck out a little. We became skilled at making things. The curtains we had brought in our suitcases became new clothes; blankets became winter coats. My mother liked knitting, and was very good at it. From my grandmother I got the samples and patterns of knitting and crochet that my mother had made. I have kept an embroidered dress made from blue curtains, and a dress that my mother knitted for herself.

My mother wanted to take me to the theatre. There was a performance of Johann Strauss's Vienna waltzes at the Théâtre du Châtelet. It must have been a Thursday or Saturday at the end of 1941. She was really looking forward to it. Light music wasn't really her thing, but it reminded her of the past. My mother would have been very disappointed if I hadn't been able to go – but that day I had a very bad cold. She had made such an effort to get the two tickets and she asked me to go with her all the same, since she didn't want to go with grandmother and leave me in the apartment on my own. So I went, but didn't enjoy it at all. The atmosphere was menacing. I felt it might have been dangerous for us to be there. And then the music was from another age and I didn't like it. It left a bitter taste, and I never went back to that theatre.

I remember one winter evening when mother and I were going home. She was elegantly dressed, as ever, with a little turquoise wool hat, and matching woolen gloves and scarf over a black coat. It must have been cold. Since the neighborhood garden square was closed off, we went along the pavement where there was a big heap of sand, probably for the paths in the garden. We didn't see it in the dark, and tripped and fell on the sand. I was amused but my mother wasn't. We dusted off our clothes, felt our way round it and went quickly home.

1942 (January to July): a black year

20 January 1942 was the date of the infamous Wannsee Conference, where the "Final solution to the Jewish problem" was drawn up. Eichmann organized the deportations from every part of Europe to the concentration camps, the death camps. He had the Nazi representatives in the territories under occupation conduct the mass arrests and organize the convoys to Auschwitz, which had been opened on 26 May 1940. The first convoy from Drancy left Bourget-Drancy station for the extermination camps on 27 March 1942. It was easy to arrest the Jews, especially the foreigners, since they had been obliged by law to register with the police on 3 October 1940. The register of Jews was ready, and the anti-Jewish laws became increasingly stringent, month by month.

The restrictions included a curfew for the Jews. The 6th edict, issued by the Nazis and the French on 7 February 1942, said "Jews may not leave their dwellings between 20h00 and 06h00", and "Jews may not change their place of residence"[11].

My mother had explained to me what the curfew meant: I had to be home by 8 o'clock. I had my watch, and I had to obey. She never said to me "If you don't come home you might be taken away"; she just let me know that walking around Paris was becoming less and less possible. I didn't ask questions because I sensed the danger in the air. But why was it dangerous? Was it because we were foreign? Or because we were Jewish? I didn't know, I mixed the two together, but I knew that I mustn't venture far from the nest late in the day. But I was just a little girl…

I still don't like to recall this incident. For once, I was playing at a school friend's house. She lived nearby on rue

---

[11] Les Juifs sous l'Occupation, Recueil des textes officiels français et allemands 1940-1944, Fils et filles de déportés juifs de France – F.F.D.J.F., 1982.

Charlot. I remember that on her bed she had a pillowslip with Mickey Mouse on it; that was the first time I'd seen Mickey Mouse, who was not so common in France in those days. I don't know if it was because I was at her house or because we were engrossed in our games that I didn't notice the time. It was after half past eight when I got home, to find my mother tearful and distressed and my grandmother very angry. Mother was stricken with pain, and was crying. I was so sad that I didn't even feel the spanking my grandmother gave me with an umbrella she found behind the door. I really deserved it; I think it was the only time it ever happened.

The noose tightens for the Jews

> *8th edict of measures against the Jews, May 29, 1942, entry into force June 7, 1942:*
> *I. No Jew over the age of six may appear in public without wearing the Jewish star.*
> *II. The Jewish star is a six-pointed star the size of the palm of the hand, with a black border. It is made of yellow cloth and bears the inscription "Jew" in black letters. It must be worn in a clearly visible way on the left side of the chest, firmly sewn to the garment."*

Since I was over six, I had to wear the "Jewish star". Until that point the French population in general had been indifferent to the fate that the race laws reserved for the Jews. They were thinking about their own problems, supplies, prisoners of war, and the presence of an army of occupation. This changed when they saw us wearing that yellow star with the word "JEW" on it. Some non-Jewish French people went so far as to wear a similar star with the word "GOY" on it, or "SOUTHERNER" or "SWING". They were arrested and interned in camps for a few weeks[12].

Mother and grandmother obeyed the law. They always wore that sign on their clothing. Three of them had to be bought, and they cost a point on the cloth ration! For practical reasons my mother sewed each star onto cloth lining, attaching snaps to the points so the star could be worn with all clothing[13]. I neither showed nor hid my star; I wore a scarf over it, or I folded it down if it was on a collar. In that way, if I was arrested, I couldn't be accused of not wearing it. If I saw the Gestapo or a French policeman in the distance I put it on display. I knew that if I broke that rule I would be taken to a place and to a fate that would separate me from my mother and that made me afraid. I was afraid all the time. And I was right to be afraid.

Well after the war I started having recurrent dreams of being hunted by a uniformed Nazi who pursued me through the streets of Paris or another town. There were cars parked by the sidewalks. I was in my robe that was caught on the car fenders. I was gasping and at the last moment my dressing gown came free and I ran away again, with the uniform at my heels.

Another dream: I am in a very large, mirror-lined room and I must hide. In a corner of the room there is a man in that same uniform with boots and Nazi armbands. I can't hide because there are mirrors everywhere. I am hunted and I hide and I wake up panting with my heart racing. There is little color in the dreams other than the grey-green of the uniform and the red of the Nazi armband.

On 8 July 1942, the ninth Nazi edict was published, banning Jews from theatres and cinemas, sports ground, parks and gardens, and stores (large and small). Shopping

---

[12] Les Juifs pendant l'occupation, André Kaspi, Seuil, 1991 et 1997, p.110
[13] L'étoile des juifs, Serge Klarsfelf, l'Archipel 1992.

was permitted only between 3 and 4 o'clock in the afternoon, but markets were completely out of bounds. The list was long. In the metro, Jews were allowed to travel only in the last car. Not only could we not go out in the evenings, but we also were excluded from all public places. We had to stay at home.

One day my mother's faithful wristwatch suddenly stopped. Obviously, we couldn't have it repaired. I think that deep down she took that as a bad omen. If you rely on your watch every day, it seems like treachery if it breaks down.

When she was taken away on July 16 my mother took all her jewelry but left the watch behind. She must have thought she would be able to trade them in at that place. She took her beautiful engagement ring, a ruby set in diamonds. The Nazis did not list the valuables that deportees took with them to Drancy and Auschwitz during that particular mass arrest. I remember that ring because it had always fascinated me.

The Final Solution

Preparation for the mass arrests of 16 and 17 July 1942

On 11 June 1942, Eichmann arranged for 100,000 Jews to be deported east from France: trains, buses and policemen were made ready.

On 9 July, the delegate of the secretary for the police issued orders: "arrest and rounding up for deportation of 22,000 Jews of both sexes, between the ages of 15 and 50, of the following nationalities: German, Austrian, Polish, Czechoslovak, Russian (White and Red), and stateless people. Jews with an Aryan spouse, breastfeeding mothers and women in advanced stages of pregnancy are exempt."[14]

---

[14] Serge Klarsfeld, "Vichy-Auschwitz I (Fayard, 1983), p. 242

The Nazis themselves and other Vichy officials subsequently amended those instructions. Children under 16 were included and the age limit was raised to 55 for women and 60 for men.

Laval wrote to the Nazis that the matter of children in the occupied zone "did not interest him".[15] Besides, "some of the children under 15 registered on their parents' file might not have been arrested.[16]

16 July saw the start of what is now referred to as "the mass arrest of the Vel d'Hiv' (the Vélodrome d'Hiver -the Winter Velodrome). It was completed the following day.

The French municipal police, under the orders of Emile Hennequin, wanted to show their enthusiasm by arresting old people also and children under 16. More than four thousand children under 15 were arrested in the two days of the operation.[17] By some miracle my name was not on the July 16 list.

On July 16, 1942 there seems to have been some confusion over the appropriate age of children. Lists must have been mixed up, because Hennequin's directive stipulated that people over the age of 65 and children under 16 were also "to be taken".

For this grim business an estimated 9,000 police, gendarmes, French guards and other auxiliaries were mobilized. The police contingent of 4,660 included 2,744 regulars and 1,916 extra recruits. The gendarmes supervising the convoys used the prefectural register to arrest people.[18] In total almost 76,000 Jews were deported from France to the concentration camps by the Nazis and their French collaborators. Only 3,000 of those survived and returned. By

---

[15] Maurice Rajsfus, "La Rafle du Vel d'Hiv (P.U.F., 2002)
[16] René Rémond, "Le Fichier juif",
[17] Claude Lévy and Paul Tillard, "La Grande rafle du Vel d'Hiv'" (Robert Laffont, 1992) ; Maurice Rajsfus, op.cit.
[18] Jean Defrasne, "L'occupation allemande en France" (P.U.F., 1985)

21 July the total number of people arrested stood at 13,152: 3,118 men, 5,919 women and 4,115 children.[19]

My mother and grandmother had heard the rumors about internment camps or labor camps in Poland, but I don't think they dared contemplate the worst, the inconceivable. We were therefore forewarned but totally unprepared. Since we knew no one, we didn't know where to go. We had been in France for only two years and we had no friends. German Jews who were so well integrated into German society (like French Jews) were not at all appreciated by eastern Jews, who were more numerous in Paris. We therefore belonged to no community, and we had almost no help.

---

[19] Maurice Rajsfus, op.cit., p.52

VIII - The Arrests, the « Rafle du Vel d'Hiv » Thursday 16 July 1942

At 8 a.m., two men in beige raincoats knocked on the door of our furnished apartment on rue Caffarelli. We were already up, since we rose with the summer light. My mother opened the door.

Two Frenchmen in plain clothes came into the apartment with my mother's permission. One was holding a sheet of paper, probably a list of names. He read out only my mother's name, "Alice Deichmann". My mother answered and he told her to get her things. The other man smiled, avoiding my eyes, and turned towards the back of the door where clothes were hanging behind the curtains. They showed no emotion.

We had heard about the arrests and the three of us knew we could be interned into camps. Our suitcases were almost packed with the essentials; we just had a few things to add. That was the state we were in: ready to be led off like docile animals with no escape. We didn't know where else to go: no money, no family, no papers. Three generations caught in a trap: grandmother, mother and daughter.

My mother closed the suitcase she had taken from under the bed. I remember screaming "Mummy I want to go with you!"

The men told me my name wasn't on the list. I begged them to take me too. My mother was pale, and she only said "my darling" or "my darling, be good". She kissed me, and then she left between the two men.

I wasn't on their list, nor was grandmother. Grandmother was 62 and I was nine and a half.

Women between the ages of 15 and 55 and men between the ages of 15 and 50 were to be arrested. As we have seen, the fate of children under the age of 15 was not clear during the July 16 arrests. Some were on the lists others were not. Did those two men have a moment of weakness?

My mother's arrest took about fifteen minutes. Grandmother and I were left on our own. Grandmother, who was so strong, was stricken.

I cried for a long time when mother left, shouting "mummy, mummy!" Then I was scared and I wanted to hide. And yet I was glad to be able to stay in the room. I felt – and this troubles me to this day – I felt happy that I wasn't on the list. I wanted to be with my mother but I was glad not to have been taken, not to be going towards an unknown fate.

And that was when I started to feel a heavy burden of guilt: my mother had been arrested but not me. I have to live with that feeling; I can't root it out. I too should have died in the gas chambers; we should have died together … but I am still here.

Childhood, innocence and especially a strong survival instinct took over.

My mother was everything to me. In the circumstances she was also my memory, through all these changes and removals. She was in my bubble, a part of me; we had a very strong bond. At the same time I was very independent and often disobedient: a normal child! But if at school they had told me the world was round and she had said it was square, it's her I would have believed.

She was gentleness, the arts, and knowledge. My world collapsed on that dark day.

IX - Drancy

My mother's fate

Once the threshold crossed, my mother went downstairs and was taken to the bus that was waiting at a specific place in the arrondissement for all who had been caught in the net. The French authorities planning the arrests had reserved about fifty buses from the "Compagnie du Metropolitain". Families with children under fifteen were then sent to the Vel d'Hiv' in the 15th arrondissement of Paris. Those without children were taken to Drancy.

It was the initial census of 3 October 1940 that made the arrests possible. Every Jew arrested had a file drawn from that register, on which either "Drancy" or "Vélodrome d'Hiver" was marked for ease of verification[20].

My mother was taken to Drancy on 16 July 1942.

The camp at Drancy, a close suburb of Paris, had been set up in a residential neighborhood, in unfinished low-rent accommodations. The large, horseshoe shaped building had not been completed when war broke out. It became an internment camp in 1941, guarded by French gendarmes. It quickly became a transit camp. Of the 76,000 people deported from France to the death camps, 67,000 passed through Drancy.

The "living conditions" in Drancy were appalling. Of the 11,363 Jews arrested on that extremely hot 16 July, 6,000 were interned there. Piled 70 to 80 per room, where they slept on the floor or on mats. Food was completely inadequate. The few functioning toilets were quickly plugged. Hygienic conditions, virtually non-existent, became

---

[20] La Rafle du Vel d'hiv, Maurice Rajsfus, P.U.F., 2002, p.111

unbearable. Each of the internees suffered anguish over their fate and that of their family.

The only human touch to the rules was the authorization to send and receive two cards per month and a parcel once a week.[21] My mother was there from 16 to 29 July and she wrote us two cards – in French, so they could be checked.

In the first card, dated 21 July six days after her arrival, she said she was glad to be able to write to us and asked us to send her an unbreakable plate and a few personal effects. No food. Although the food provided at Drancy was well below survival rations, she was afraid of depriving us. On the envelope, my mother's address was "Mrs Alice Deichmann, Block II, Stair 8, room 9, Drancy/Seine". Grandmother answered her on "interzone cards" and sent her a package.

The second card, sent on 28 July was harrowing but infinitely courageous, informing us of her imminent departure. "Tomorrow we leave – perhaps to aunt Jenny's, but we don't know". This meant a work camp (as perhaps she believed) or a death camp (as was the case) in the east, to where that aunt was said to have been deported. We knew nothing of it. My mother thanked grandmother for the parcel and sent back a parcel with things she had decided she would not need. Then she tried to reassure us and tells us goodbye; we shall meet again.

That was the last card my mother signed. It was dated 28 July 1942. She was thirty-nine years old. Tragic writing in view of my mother's fate; she tried to reassure us. My grandmother recovered this card after the war and gave it to me much later.

Both cards were addressed to my grandmother at our address in rue Caffarelli. In both, my mother asked us to greet Mme Sontag, the building manager, and asked us to

---

[21] André Kaspi, "Les Juifs pendant l'occupation" (Seuil, 1991 & 1997), p.268.

show her the first card from Drancy. My mother trusted her, but I didn't. I never liked her and always thought she was pro-Nazi. To this day I do not know how or through whom my grandmother received this correspondence, because the day after mother's arrest, grandmother and I went into hiding. Helped by a man who knew my grandmother, we were hidden separately by various people.

Meanwhile in Drancy…

When a train became available, 1,000 detainees were assembled the night before it was due to leave. On 28 July my mother and her companions in sorrow were separated from the others. They got ready to leave very early the next morning. They were searched and their jewelry, money and other valuables were confiscated. They were then herded into rooms in groups of 70-80 in another part of the camp.

On 29 July at 8:35AM the Commandant of Auschwitz was told of the imminent departure of convoy number 12. My mother and the other detainees were put on buses again and taken from Drancy to Bourget station, where a train awaited: a locomotive with cattle or freight cars into which a thousand people were loaded.

Convoy number 12 of 29 July consisted of 270 men and 730 women. According to the archives and the telex sent to Berlin by the Nazis, it left at 8:55AM. Most of the deportees were between 36 and 54 years of age. My mother was among the youngest. She was 39 years old and the only German.

She then suffered the torment of the journey. There were about fifty people in each car, standing, crowded together. If they had any meager luggage, they leaned on it in the terrible heat, with neither water nor air, for sixty hours.

My mother arrived in Auschwitz on 31 July 1942.

The following sources were used: Serge Klarsfeld, "Le Calendrier"; (Fils et filles de déportés juifs de France (F.F.D.J.F.), 1993); André Kaspi, "Les Juifs pendant l'occupation" (Seuil, 1991 & 1997); Claude Lévy and Paul Tillard, « La grande rafle du Vel d'Hiv' » (Laffont, 1992) ; Serge Klarsfeld, « Vichy-Auschwitz (Fayard, 1983).

X - Auschwitz

Stepping down from the convoy number 12 on this 31 July 1942, the deportees were separated into two columns by the Nazis: those who seemed fit for work and those who seemed unfit for work and therefore unfit for life.

On arrival that day, 270 men and 514 women were selected for work and had a serial number tattooed on their arm.[22] Two hundred and sixteen women - 216 - were not tattooed but were sent immediately to the gas chambers. My mother was one of them.

The SS and their henchmen told them they were going for a shower. Each was given a towel and soap and sent to the showers. When the doors were closed behind them, Zyklon B gas was released from canisters to fill the room. For a long time I believed that that terrible death was instantaneous, but alas it was not. The agony could last ten to fifteen minutes until death: an eternity. I am obsessed by that thought, which fills me with pain. For those long minutes, people were suffocating. Since the gas came in from low vents, people pushed and climbed on top of one another in order to breathe air.

At times I try to reason and tell myself that my mother probably escaped an even harsher fate since only 5 of the thousand people in convoy 12 returned in 1945. No women survived. The probability of coming through that hell was very small. Given that so very few survived, did the gas chamber spare her the prolonged, atrocious suffering that would have come?

---

[22] Serge Klarsfeld, "Le Calendrier" (F.F.D.J.F., 1993, p.378

I try to re-live my mother's last moments, her torment and execution. Why was she murdered on arrival? She had been in very good health before the arrest. What happened to render her unfit for work at 39? Had she contracted dysentery or some other disease at Drancy? The handwriting on her cards from there were normal, not the writing of a sick person.

Crowded together in the wagon with others, sometimes I imagine she died on the train, and that her body was removed… but it is much more likely that she was sent to the gas chamber.

One thing I am sure of, which may explain that immediate execution, is that the Nazis wanted to eliminate the German Jews first, whom they regarded as "the worst".

I will never have more precise answers. My mother died that day.

XI - Wandering

Late in the afternoon of the day my mother was arrested, a friend of my grandmother came to warn us of imminent danger.

He was a German Jew, a grey-haired man who may have been living in France for a long time and who was part of the network to save Jews and protect foreigners. He was no doubt part of the Comité d'Assistance aux Réfugiés, C.A.R., an organization founded in 1936 to help German Jews.

He came to tell us that we absolutely could not stay there. He must have had detailed information about the mass arrests planned for 16 and 17 July. He insisted that we leave our apartment that very day, otherwise we would be arrested the next day, he told us. He had found two hiding places, for grandmother and for me. I never saw that man again.

We took what my mother had left and our personal effects, which did not amount to much. To be expected, we never recovered the possessions we had left in rue Caffarelli. We took some clothes and some valuables. Each of us took our suitcase and went our separate way.

From that day onwards I never wore again the Jewish star, which I detested, as all Jews did. I never changed my name in all my wanderings. No one asked or told me to change identity or to invent a life story. If the Gestapo were to check my identity, I would be deported and killed.

When the anti-Jewish laws were first promulgated, the French had remained passive, or outright informers or collaborators, but when Jews were made to wear the star, a clandestine resistance movement was created in the French population. People were horrified and moved to pity by the arrest of women and children in particular. A rare few members of the Catholic clergy such as Monsignor Saliège of Toulouse, and a larger number of protestant ministers, called openly for solidarity with the Jews. And Jewish movements took action when they could. Individuals and entire villages concealed and fed Jewish people; one example was Le Chambon-sur-Lignon, with the advice of Pastor Trocmé and his wife. There was also Alice Ferrières, who set up a rescue network in the Midi-Pyrénées region. Others formed lay or religious mutual support groups, which saved children.

The « CIMADE » was a committee in which Madeleine Barot was very active in helping Jewish children and adults to cross the border into Switzerland. Another one was "Entraide temporaire", an association for the protection of Jewish children that saved 500 children in the Paris area, thanks in particular to Denise and Fred Milhaud. In the latter support group were many social workers who individually took the children to the families where they would be hidden and saw to it that their stipend be paid. Marthe Laborde was one of them. She was a social worker at the Créteil hospital. She saved my life.

There were also the Jewish Scouts of France and the General Union of French Jews, though unfortunately the latter was under Vichy control, so somewhat double-edged.[23]

A woman from Alsace who lived in Vanves, a suburb of Paris, hid grandmother. She did business with the Germans. Grandmother lived there with her from July 1942 until the Liberation of Paris in August 1944. She helped in the house and with her activities. Grandmother never spoke ill of her, except to say that she engaged in black-marketeering with the Germans, which she did not approve of. But it was a matter of life or death. Grandmother told me that often she

---

[23] See Hélène Berr, "Journal" (Tallandier, 2008); Patrick Cabanel, "Chère Mademoiselle" (Calmann-Lévy, 2010) ; Collective authorship, « Traqués, Cachés, Vivants » (L'Harmattan, 2004) ; Patrick Cabanel, Histoire des Justes de France (Armand Collin, 2012), André Jacques, « Madeleine Barot »,(Cerf, 1989)

did not hide from German soldiers since the woman passed her off as a family member. I know that grandmother also spoke with some soldiers – not the Nazis, but the Wehrmacht. The German occupiers were well disposed towards the woman, and grandmother did not match the racial stereotypes that the population was fed with. She may have used her maiden name, Bock, which was a mediaeval German name, and perhaps concocted a life story with the agreement of her host.

I stayed in Paris until early 1943. I lost all track of time, everything was up in the air: my mother was gone, and there was no school. I no longer knew what day it was. I hardly ever went out.

First I was in a young family – at least they gave me the impression of being younger than my mother. I didn't stay there long, perhaps a week. Then I was with some lovely people who were very kind to me. I don't recall what that young couple looked like just that their apartment was dark and that I slept on two chairs put end to end. I still remember how uncomfortable it was. Those first two hiding places were not far from rue Caffarelli.

Right before or right after that I stayed briefly in a summer camp for children, not far from Paris. I was so hungry! I made friends with another little girl whose face I can't recall, my only brief friendship in that period, and who was as hungry as I was. We gathered wild plums from the bushes that divided the fields. They were very bitter, but they got better after the first frost. They soothed my stomach cramps for a time.

Then I was moved to 4 rue Balzac in the 8th arrondissement, where I stayed with a milliner; I was made to deliver hats and shoes throughout Paris. That must have been September 1942. It can't have been cold since I was still wearing summer dresses. I was not yet ten years old.

The woman, Renée Martin, had bought the business from Fanny Berger – real name Odette Bernstein – who was obliged to let it go for next to nothing because of the anti-Jewish laws, the Aryanization and the looting of Jewish goods. As in Germany in 1934, the law of 2 June 1941 and the edict of 28 July 1941 banned Jews from professions and from ownership of shops or businesses. A "provisional administrator" was appointed to oversee the accounts and estimate the value of the commerce, which was then sold off cheap or to the highest bidder. That was how Renée Martin bought the business for the ridiculous sum of 7,000 francs.[24] She was a coarse, hard woman. She had a Jewish partner who had left or gone into hiding; I never met him.

Fanny Berger's apartment included the workshop, which I don't remember, and the showroom. The living quarters and the large salon/showroom were luxurious, with beige and pink satin and beautiful furniture. There was an entrance, a large bedroom and a little bedroom where I slept. There was also a big kitchen, and a bathroom and toilet. I stayed for five or six weeks. She carried on making hats and she sold shoes. High heels were in fashion; my mother never wore them, and I had probably inherited some of my grandmother's prejudices on the subject. How could you walk in such things? I probably thought that decent women wouldn't wear them.

Customers were brought into the showroom; I saw their silhouettes, because obviously I wasn't allowed out. The milliner often went out during the day to sell her merchandise. I was told not to answer the telephone. There was a blind man one floor above us. He tapped with his white cane, sometimes on the front door. I was terrified.

I wandered from one room to the next with a little black suitcase. It contained just a few clothes and a doll – the only object that linked me to my previous existence and to my

---

[24] See the documentary film "Assassinat d'une modiste", by Catherine Bernstein, produced jointly by ARTE France and IO Productions (2005)

mother. I must have chosen it carefully from among the others. The woman told me not to play during the day: "Leave your doll: you can't play. There's work to be done!"

The Parisian wartime diet was not balanced. I had trouble with my digestion and she listened to what I was doing. If I spent five minutes too long in the toilet she would say "Why are you staying so long in the toilet?" It was humiliating.

She would speak harshly with me: "Go and get this, do that!" I had to run errands, buying milk and bread, and delivering hats. One day when she sent me to buy milk I ran away. It was the only hiding place I ran away from, the only time I suffered in my wanderings. I ran off because it was as if that milliner was beating me, mentally. Running away was a terrible risk. I didn't grasp how dangerous it was.

With the money for the milk, I took the metro and went to see a hatter to whom I had made one or two deliveries. She had a shop on the rue du Faubourg St Antoine near the St Paul metro station.

She must have felt sorry for me. She was the first woman to touch me since my mother left; she was very kind to me and I was very fond of her; there was something motherly about her. Her husband was Jewish and he had been arrested. I immediately told her what was wrong and begged her to keep me. She told me she could put me up that night, but that she couldn't keep me longer. The situation was as dangerous for her as for me.

I had nothing but the clothes I was dressed in. Her house was quite far out in the suburbs. It seemed like heaven to me. It was a house on several floors, on its own, by a big field. The lady had a daughter who was younger than me. You could hear the trains passing not far off. I stayed only one or two days.

During the night, waking or sleeping, and at dusk, I heard a train in the distance, and a dog barking nearby. I associate those two sounds with well-being and the realization that the situation couldn't last; I knew that I had to leave that place for an uncertain future. Today still, when I hear a train or a dog barking in the distance, I am reminded of it. Years later I looked for that woman again, but her shop doesn't exist anymore.

After that brief interlude with the hatter I had to return to the milliner, who screamed at me "You are so stupid! You're like a donkey! It was idiotic to run away!" I wept and had to apologize. She had the bright idea of punishing me by not taking me back.

A social worker from a help network brought me to another home in Créteil, in a suburban villa where a kind couple of pensioners lived with their granddaughter, who was my age. We played together a lot. There was a large, well-tended garden with flagstone paths and a stone bordered raised bed with aromatic herbs that we tasted. I still remember the taste of sorrel. At the time there were still a few farms near Créteil. I was often sent with the pail to get milk after the cows had been milked in the late afternoon or early evening. The little girl seldom came with me. I wasn't afraid of the dark, and I took a short cut through a small cemetery. One evening, in the warm air of summer's end, with no streetlight nearby, I saw little blue flames coming out of the ground in different parts of the graveyard. They disappeared quickly. I never told anyone, in case they laughed at me. It was only much later that I understood that this was methane from decomposing organic matter. Mine was a solitary childhood.

Once again I was not getting enough to eat, and the couple couldn't keep me, probably because they didn't have enough food. And it could be that they couldn't look after a second child. I must have stayed there a month.

It was many years later that I learned the name of the social worker who took care of me: Melle Marthe Laborde. She was one of those heroic people who saved Jewish children from going to the death camps. Through her work at the Hospital in Créteil, she managed to find families in the

French provinces, well outside the Paris region, who would take these children. Melle Laborde alone « placed » over 207 Jewish children throughout rural France.

After my last hiding place in Créteil, she took me to her home in Saint-Maur, a lovely house with gravel paths. It was an impressive place. Her mother and sister-in-law, a beautiful woman, met us at the front steps. The memory of that welcome stays with me like a photograph. I stayed there for two days, until Melle Laborde found me another hiding place. I would have loved to stay with them in this small château, but that was not possible. It was much too dangerous.

Every stay was short – from a night to a month. I often heard people say, "We would like to do more but we can't". All those people were wonderful to me, but they couldn't keep me. Perhaps they were fearful of being denounced. It was a chain of friendly human care, broken only by the milliner. I was hunted, and moved on. No sooner had I made friends with people than I had to leave again; another bond was broken.

During these seven or eight months I was in an altered state, adrift, without the guidance of my mother. I was taken from place to place like an object, a little creature withdrawn into its shell. I stayed for so short a time in some places that I have forgotten them completely. I was aware of the courage of people risking their life to hide me. But it was somehow anonymous, in that I never stayed long enough with people to form a lasting bond. There were many of them, and I have forgotten many, being too traumatized. I was in hiding and I did not ask questions.

A few abused the children entrusted to them. Though I encountered one "wicked stepmother" in the course of my wandering, all without exception risked their lives. It is to those people with "intelligent hearts" as my mother would have said, that I owe my life. I survived thanks to them.

Without them, all or nearly all the Jews in France would have perished. Three-quarters survived.

From one temporary hiding place to the next I went until the beginning of 1943, when I left Paris.

" Opa " (grandfather), Isidor Aron, identity photo for an official document, Sarrebrücken, Germany, around 1935

With aunt Ida while visiting Saarbrücken, Germany, 16 April 1938

With uncle Erich while visiting Remich, Luxembourg, 1934

With grandmother and mother, Saarbrücken, Germany, January 1936

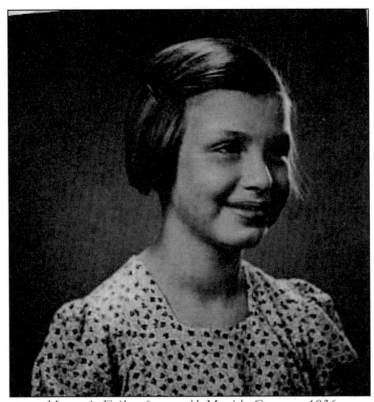

My cousin Erika, 6 years old, Munich, Germany, 1936

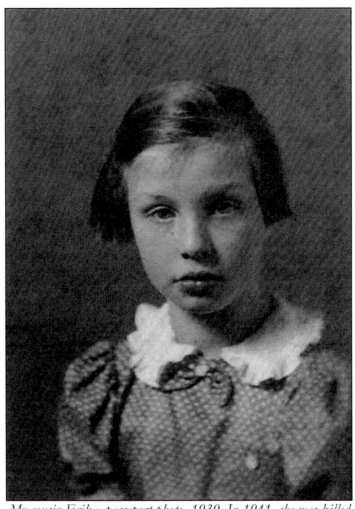
My cousin Erika, passeport photo, 1939. In 1941, she was killed with her parents in Kaunas, Lithuania

Record from Buchenwald indicating that grandfather Ivan Deichmann is freed, 22 November 1938

With mother, Luxembourg, July 1939

Page of aunt Ida's passport with a visa for China, 1940

```
NOM : DEICHMANN née Aron
PRÉNOMS : Alice
Date et lieu de naissance : 30.6.1903 à Nuremberg
                                      N° du Dossier juif : 1741
SEXE : Féminin
NATIONALITÉ : Allemande
PROFESSION : Sans
ADRESSE : 12, Rue Caffarelli

SITUATION de famille : Marié
CONJOINT : Juif
                    Prénoms        | Date et lieu de naissance | Nationalité
ENFANTS    Marion                  | 18.11.1932                | Weiblith
de moins   Béatrice
de 15 ans
et à charge

INFIRMITÉS :

SERVICES de GUERRE :
Convoi 29-7-42

SITUATION
administrative
de l'étranger

N° du casier central :
REMARQUES PARTICULIÈRES :
Arrêtée le 16-7-42
```

Civil record from the Paris police headquarters, 1940

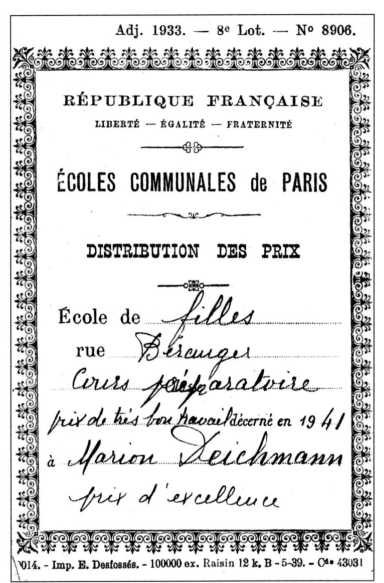

First school year in France, Paris, July 1941

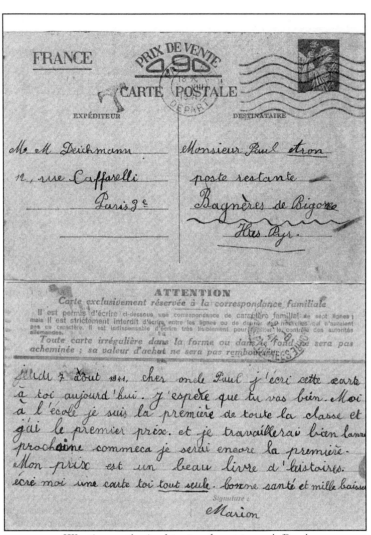

*Wartime authorized postcard sent to uncle Paul,
in hiding 1941*

Uncle Paul, Bagnères de Bigorre, 1942

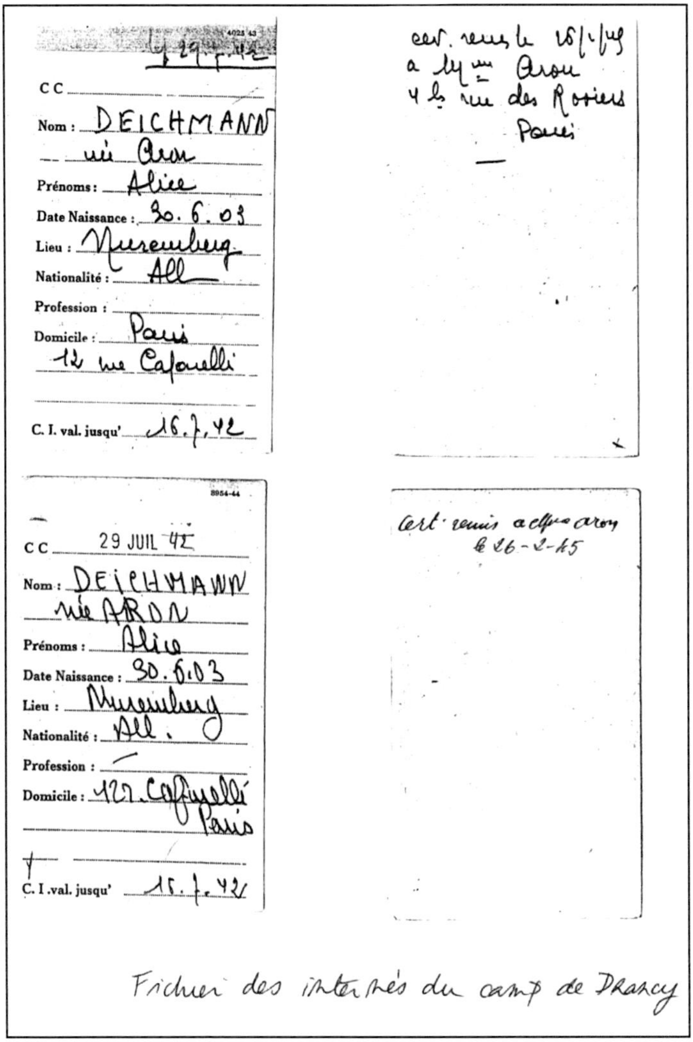

4025 43

4 29.7.42

CC

Nom : DEICHMANN

née Aron

Prénoms : Alice

Date Naissance : 30.6.03

Lieu : Nuremberg

Nationalité : All

Profession :

Domicile : Paris

12 rue Caffarelli

C. I. val. jusqu' 16.7.42

cert. remis le 18/1/49
à Mme Aron
4 bis rue des Rosiers
Paris

8954-44

CC 29 JUIL 42

Nom : DEICHMANN

née ARON

Prénoms : Alice

Date Naissance : 30.6.03

Lieu : Nuremberg

Nationalité : All.

Profession : —

Domicile : 12 r. Caffarelli

Paris

C. I .val. jusqu' 16.7.42

cert. remis à Mme Aron
le 26-2-45

Fichier des internés du camp de Drancy

Mother interned in Drancy from 16 through 29 July 1942

Camp de Drancy, 21.7.42.

Ma chère mère, ma chère petite Marion!
Quelle joie aujourd'hui, je peux vous écrire
quelques mots. Je me trouve bien - et
j'espère de tout mon cœur, que vous
deux, mes très chères, vous êtes aussi
en bonne santé. Écrivez moi s.v.p.
toute de suite sur une carte interzone
comme vous allez. Avec tous mes
pensées je suis toujours avec vous.
Aussi vous pouvez m'envoyer un petit
colis avec des vêtements: alors, chère mère,
envoie la robe bleue marine (tricotée)
et la robe d'été à rayure, la blouse à rayure
et encore 2 culottes,

blanche - rouge, une serviette éponge. Comme
vaisselle une assiette incassable, mais
n'envoyez rien à manger. On en a assez
ici. Nous sommes encore ici, mais on ne
sait pas, si c'est pour longtemps. Il faut
toujours espérer et on se reverra un
jour. Restez moi en bonne santé. - Si tu
n'as pas assez d'argent, chère mère, tu
peux vendre quelques choses inutiles. -
Alors, mes très chères, portez vous bien et
soyez courageuses. Mille baisers pour
ma petite Schnaffi, - pour toi, chère
maman!   Toujours votre Alice.

Faites voir cette carte à Mme Sontag, dites lui
beaucoup des bonnes choses et je suis toujours
reconnaissante pour sa bonté.

First letter from mother, Drancy, 21 July 1942

Drancy, 28/7/42

Ma chère Mère, ma chère petite Marion, ma chère!
Je suis tellement heureuse d'avoir
les nouvelles de vous douze, mes chères, aussi
le colis j'ai reçu, merci beaucoup.
J'espère, vous allez bien, moi aussi
je suis en bonne santé. Demain nous
partons - peut-être chez Tante Jenny, on
ne sait rien. Mais faites pas des mau-
vaises sens de tout ça. Je vous donne
des nouvelles aussitôt que possible.
Restez moi en bonne santé - et ayez
toujours courage. On se reverra ! -
J'espère, tu as des nouvelles de Paul, chère
maman. Il sait déjà, que je suis ici ?
J'ai déjà trouvé beaucoup des amis ici
Aujourd'hui j'ai renvoyé un colis avec des
objets inutiles pour moi - mais peut-être
pas pour vous. - Alors, mes très chères
restez moi toujours en bonne santé
avec toutes mes pensées, avec tout
mon coeur je suis toujours chez
vous ! - Je t'embrasse, ma petite
et chère maman et mille baisers !
                                    Votre Aline

Second and last sign of life from my mother in Drancy on the eve of departure for Auschwitz, 29 July 1942

Mr Parigny, Michel, Daniel, Marion and Claudine, St Hilaire du Harcouët, April 1944

Marion and friend, First Communion, St Hilaire du Harcouët, September 1944

Parigny Family, St Hilaire du Harcouët, 1947

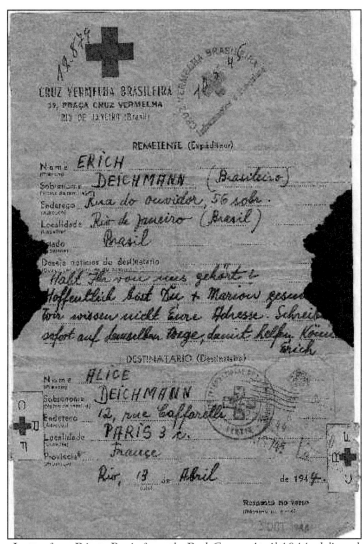

Letter from Rio to Paris from the Red Cross, April 1944, delivered November 1944

With grandmother and uncle Paul, Paris, July 1945

S. E. R.

SIÈGE CENTRAL:
**23, Boulevard Haussmann
PARIS**
Tél. : PRO. 99.90 - 91 - 92 - 93

Réf. à rappeler :

JR/J 5935/R. 15077

Le 30 Octobre 45

Monsieur Paul ARON
51, rue de Malte
P A R I S .
-:-:-:-:-:-:-:-:-:-:-:-.

Monsieur,

    Comme suite à la visite que vous avez faite à nos bureaux pour nous demander des renseignements au sujet de :

        Mme DEICHMANN Alice née ARON
        née le 30.6.03 à Nuremberg
        dernière adresse : 12, rue Cafarelli

nous avons le regret de vous faire savoir qu'elle a été déportée le 29.7.42 du camp de DRANCY en direction d'AUSCHWITZ.

    Ne trouvant pas son nom sur les listes de libérés que nous possèdons, nous ne manquerons pas de porter à votre connaissance toute nouvelle que nous pourrions recevoir à son sujet.

    Entretemps, nous vous prions de croire, Monsieur, à l'assurance de nos sentiments les plus dévoués.

First negative response to our search to find my mother

« The two last signs of life from our unforgettable Alice », written by my grandmother on the envelop containing the two cards from Drancy

COMITÉ INTERGOUVERNEMENTAL POUR LES RÉFUGIÉS
DÉLÉGATION POUR LA FRANCE

PARIS
77, AV. DES CHAMPS-ÉLYSÉES

TÉLÉPHONE : ÉLY 62-53
— 54-64
— 69-07

N° 9394
F.SO

Par application
du décret en date du 10 Mai 1945
Journal Officiel n° 182 du 4 Août 1945

CERTIFICAT

PARIS, LE 23 Janvier 1946

Nous Gouverneur V. VALENTIN-SMITH,
DÉLÉGUÉ POUR LA FRANCE DU COMITÉ INTERGOUVERNEMENTAL POUR LES RÉFUGIÉS
SUR DEMANDE DE Monsieur Paul ARON Tuteur de Mlle Marion
DEMEURANT DEICHMANN, sa nièce.
38, Rue d'Hulm PARIS.-(8°)

CERTIFIONS :

- que des pièces produites par lui, il résulte que Mademoiselle Marion DEICHMANN née le 18 Novembre 1932 à KARLSRUHE (Allemagne) fille de Kurt DEICHMANN et de son épouse Alice née ARON, d'origine allemande de descendance israélite, est réfugiée provenant d'Allemagne ne pouvant justifier d'aucune nationalité, visée par l'article I de la Convention de Genève du 10 Février 1938 (J.O.du 4 Août 1945 - N°182) concernant le Statut des Réfugiés provenant d'Allemagne et se trouve sous mandat du COMITE INTERGOUVERNEMENTAL POUR LES REFUGIES.

EN FOI DE QUOI le présent certificat lui est délivré pour être joint à sa demande à sa demande en délivrance d'un "Titre de voyage" lui permettant de se rendre aux ETATS-UNIS.

Le Délégué :

Gouverneur V. VALENTIN-SMITH.

Intergovernmental Committee for Refugees travel certificate, for immigration to the United States, January 1946. Origin and religion are noted

Marion carrying the sign « France » during the French scout parade, New York, USA, April 1948

(CG)

MINISTÈRE
DES ANCIENS COMBATTANTS
ET VICTIMES DE LA GUERRE.

DIRECTION
DES PENSIONS
ET DES SERVICES MÉDICAUX.

SOUS-DIRECTION
DES PENSIONS.

5 Bureau.

Rue de Bercy, n° 139,
Paris (XII°).

N° 9011
D.P.   S/▼C

RÉPUBLIQUE FRANÇAISE.

Paris, le 28 SEPT. 1953

LE MINISTRE DES ANCIENS COMBATTANTS
ET VICTIMES DE GUERRE

à

Monsieur CARON Paul
900 Riverside Drive
NEW - YORK 32, N.Y
(U.S.A.)

Monsieur,

Par lettre en date du 14 AOUT 1953, vous me demandez quelles sont les réparations auxquelles vous pouvez prétendre du fait que vous avez votre nièce à votre charge depuis la déportation de sa mère.

J'ai l'honneur de vous faire connaitre que la loi N° 46-III7 du 20 Mai 1946, régit les réparations à accorder aux victimes civiles de la guerre de nationalité française.

Les réfugiés dits " Réfugiés Statutaires " peuvent se prévaloir des dispositions de la dite loi, s'ils sont domiciliés en FRANCE.

En conséquence, et dans le cas où l'orpheline DEICHMANN serait de nationalité française, il vous appartient si vous êtes le tuteur, de vous adresser à Mr. le Consul de France de votre domicile en vue de constituer un dossier de demande de pension d'orpheline de victime civile de la guerre à son profit.

Veuillez agréer Monsieur, l'assurance de ma considération distinguée.

Pour le Ministre des Anciens Combattants
et Victimes de Guerre et par son ordre
Pour le Directeur des Pensions
et des Services Médicaux,
Le Chef du Bureau.

Request for aid by uncle Paul to the French Government, refused for no longer residing in France, New York, 1953

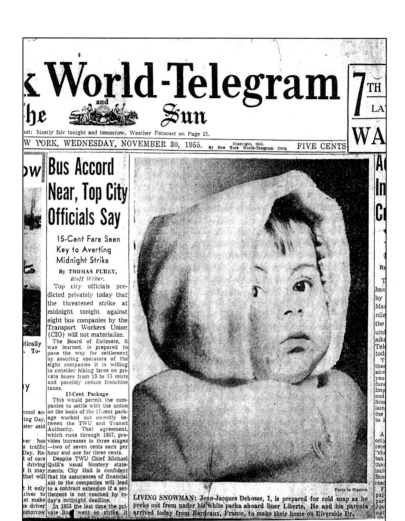

Arrival in New York : our son John is on the front page of the New York World Telegram, 30 November 1955

The two brothers : my father Kurt (87 years old) and uncle Erich (89 years old) in front of the pastry shop, Rio, Brazil, 21 September 1994

Marion Deichmann in 2015

XII - Normandy, February or March 1943 to December 1944

Melle Laborde and I made a very long journey one morning in the winter of 1943. I was outwardly calm, but inside I was very worried. The buses that we took were cold and uncomfortable. We crossed unfamiliar country.

Another world opened up to me. I had not left Paris since I'd arrived in France. Destiny took me to St. Hilaire du Harcouët in the department of La Manche. It was a small provincial town in Normandy, a province rich in history. The town was at the confluence of two rivers, and at the crossroads of two main roads: Caen-Rouen and Paris-Saint-Malo, not far from the Mont St. Michel

La Manche was extremely rural, though close to the sea. I ended up in a landscape typical of the Norman countryside: fields of wheat and buckwheat enclosed by hedgerows, with shrubs growing amongst them. Along the hedges were paths, often lower than the fields. Apple trees everywhere, not yet in blossom at the time of my arrival. In spring there was a marvelous profusion of flowers. The air in Normandy smelled so soft and soothing, far from Paris and all that was familiar. It was the start of a new life.

I was warmly welcomed – I could almost say rescued – by a "complete" family, the Parigny family. The father's name was François, the mother's Angèle. They had two sons and one daughter. The older son was Michel (probably 14 or 15 years old), then Claudine (one year older than me, that is to say 11 years old), and Daniel, 9 years old. From the point of view of age and gender, I fitted perfectly into this family.

Claudine was cheerful and lively, Michel was serious, and Daniel liked to play all the time. M. Parigny had light green eyes and was a fine looking man. He had a mustache and salt and pepper hair. I rarely saw him without his navy blue beret. He was serious and sweet and well respected in the community. He had fought at Verdun and detested the Germans, never pronouncing the word "Germans", always calling them "boches".

There was a small group of resistance members at St. Hilaire. I suspect that M. Parigny was a member of that local group ... I never really knew. He was definitely anti-Nazi.

Mme Parigny was good looking also – tall with a smiling face and fine, regular features, long chestnut hair which she twisted and put up in a bun at the back of her head. She had a well-rounded matronly figure.

The mother was stricter than the father; she was in charge of running the house. I was totally accepted by all of them, including the children, and integrated completely into the family. Apart from one incident at the beginning, I was never reprimanded or rather I was treated like the children of the family.

The Parignys were not intellectuals, but they were educated. They owned a café, bar and tobacco store on the rue de Mortain right in the center of St Hilaire and its Place Nationale. Their business was well run and popular. The front of the store took up the entire width of the house. There was a large sign "bar – café – tabac". On both sides of the entrance were large windows. The café had two rows of tables on the right and one on the left. The tables and chairs were of wood. The counter was at the back with the electric coffee machines behind it. It was heated by wood and coal. Sometimes, to have fun, Claudine and I would help or serve at tables during the holidays. The men often drank their coffee with a shot of calvados early in the morning before setting off for work.

There were flush toilets at the back, across a yard. The family kitchen was at the back of the café, on the ground floor. The building had three floors, the top one being the attic. The children's rooms were on the second floor. Claudine and I slept in a large bed. You needed a wooden footstool to climb into those Norman beds they were so high. There was no running water and the bedrooms were not heated. We had a pitcher of water in the bedroom that froze on cold winter nights. The fine living room was on the first floor.

Well after the war, Claudine told me that the Wehrmacht had requisitioned a room in the attic and the Parignys had to put up a soldier for a few months. He must have been very discreet, as I have no recollection of him.

I was not really hidden, or at least I didn't feel hidden, unlike the previous places I had lived. I had an active life and I participated in the life of the community like the other children.

Claudine and I attended the catholic school of the Immaculate Conception run by the Carmelite nuns. I liked those sisters a lot and I think they liked me in return. They had stiffly starched headdresses that made it difficult to kiss them on the cheek! The three that took care of me – two teachers and the principal, were very kind. I was in the same class as Claudine and a better pupil. But she never resented me for it. She wasn't the least bit jealous. But it embarrassed me a little.

We had enough to eat. Food rationing was mostly on sugar, chocolate and coffee. We had ersatz or substitute chocolate, which we sprinkled on bread for our afternoon snack. This false powdered cocoa, if it wasn't mixed in properly with the butter on our bread went up our noses: funny and painful!

Shortages affected paper, fabrics, clothes and in particular shoes a lot more. One incident that happened not long after I arrived involved the total lack of toilet paper. We cut up newspapers. I was not used to that at all…. So I found a sheet of white paper somewhere. Unfortunately it was a bill…. Mme Parigny was very upset and said things to me that hurt me, such as "If I'd known, I wouldn't have let you come". Thus I was afraid of her – her own children were too! But that didn't affect me for too long, I was just somewhat bruised… She did not hold it against me. Madame Parigny calmed down and things went well from then on. The Parignys had courage, for they didn't know what they were getting into, in taking a little Parisian girl into their family.

Some of their family members worked on the land and shared their harvests with them when they were good. However farmers were heavily taxed on their crops in the form of requisitioning by German soldiers, who regularly went round the farms and took away their quota. One day, with Claudine and Daniel, we went to the slaughterhouse to buy some meat. We were given a glass of blood – still warm – to drink. Supposedly this was to strengthen our bones. I had a terrible feeling of disgust and just managed not to vomit. I've never liked eating meat.

The children drank apple cider just after it was pressed. With meals, apart from water, we drank hard cider, which was not very sweet. Anyway, I was never hungry and had plenty to eat. There was enough, because the countryside was very close to the town: there was continuity between the two, surrounded by farms. The family had a vegetable garden a couple of kilometers away. The farms of the uncles and aunts seemed vast. I remember one estate with its chapel, outside oven and its farm buildings.

As Claudine was taller than me I was given some of her clothes. I had a pair of laced up boots with wooden soles. They became soon very worn down. I also wore Norman sabots, or wooden shoes. We wore slippers or socks inside, or straw. I had to learn how to walk in them. Sometimes I hit myself on the ankles. It was very painful, like a bolt of lightening through the flesh! It could break the skin and bleed.

As everywhere in France, there were outside toilets for men, urinals called "Vespasienne", but nothing at all for women. The latter found other solutions. In fact, in the garden behind the church, women, dressed in black, just squatted down when they needed to. I was told that they wore a style of underpants that were open in the middle. This was the custom of many of the countrywomen at the time.

Saint-Hilaire-du-Harcouët was well known for its weekly markets, in particular the farmers market. There was also a country fair at St Martin, which lasted three days and drew impressively large crowds.

On the other hand, we were rather restricted in movement. There was no gasoline available. In fact M. Parigny had a car with no tires in his garage. The Germans had confiscated most of the bicycles, although I think that he had hidden one.

For Christmas, at the beginning of December 1943 we went to church to see the Christmas manger. Even the simplest Nativity scenes had figures of Joseph, Mary, a donkey, a bull, a shepherd and the cradle of the little Jesus with its straw. But no baby. The baby only appeared at the midnight mass on Christmas Eve. That night, we put our wooden shoes in front of the fireplace before going to mass. In the morning they were full of sweets.

In Normandy, I didn't encounter any anti-Semitism except one time, from a child.

We were playing by the fountain in the main square. And there a small boy of my own age said "You're Jewish – but you don't have horns!". It didn't upset me, because I said to myself "this boy is stupid, He is mad!" I was flabbergasted that he had believed such "publicity". The description of a Jew as a devil with horns and a tail was not new to me. I had seen anti-Semitic posters during the war and I suspected that he had also seen this kind of image. Had he perhaps also heard remarks made by adults? No doubt. Some people in the village knew that I was a little Jewish refugee.

Mme Parigny was a practicing catholic, M. Parigny not. I was baptized and then did the preparation and took my first communion in September 1944. I was very happy. I was just like the others. In my mind, in having me baptized, Mme Parigny had saved my soul. But perhaps it was also to help me to blend in.

I was a catholic for a little while, and then I went back to Paris. I went twice to mass at Saint Paul's church, on rue des Rosiers. My uncle made no objection. I had not been raised in the Jewish faith. I had of course attended Jewish Seders but I only knew the major festivals such as Kippur, Hanukkah and Pessah. Hanukkah, the festival of lights, was the most important to me, and it was always linked to Christmas.

Catholicism also remained very superficial; I didn't believe in it deeply. The most important things were the feasts and the beautiful church of St. Hilaire. I was very pleased with my beautiful white communion dress; it was like playing at being brides. I believed, but not deeply. There was no problem of identity for me and as a child of 10 or 11 years old, I felt no confusion.

One of the Parigny great-aunts, aunt Anaïse was a non-believer! She laughed and mocked when we went to church. She said to us, Claudine and I, "you're going to church again? Are you going to see the little saint that pees?" She was referring to the statue of a little angel. I thought aunt Anaïse was particularly fun and amusing.

The two grandmothers, Parigny and Vaudouer (the mother of Mme Parigny) were still alive and we saw them often. They were kind and all shriveled up. As widows, they always wore black: from the apron to the dress, to the headdress. Except for Sunday when they went to mass, then the headdress was white.

I led a relatively normal life in St. Hilaire. In spite of being far from my family, I had found a certain sense of well-being. However, the major strategic event of that war was going to change our daily lives: the landings of allied troops in Normandy!

A few days after the landings on 6 June 1944, leaflets were dropped from planes over St Hilaire, to warn the population to leave the town. The leaflets said that in order to dislodge the enemy the allied forces would have to attack the area we were living in. It was therefore vital to evacuate. Some townspeople unfortunately stayed where they were. Thanks to the farsightedness of Mr Parigny and no doubt also to his experience in World War I, we all left together, on foot, carrying our suitcases and pushing a wheelbarrow full of clothes, food, and a few precious possessions. We walked along a hilly road for a dozen kilometers, towards Saint-Brice-de-Landelles.

Exodus to the farm (June – August 1944)

Mr. Parigny had a large family and we went to the home of one of his brothers, not far from Saint-Brice, on a small farm. All the men were gone; they had been taken prisoner. The women were left to run the farms themselves and they helped each other.

From the first day of the landings, on 6 June, single planes bombed the railway station at St. Hilaire. There was considerable material damage but no casualties.

It was on 14 June at 8.10 pm precisely that the allies bombarded the town with incendiary bombs and it was 80% destroyed. The houses still standing no longer had windows or doors, and the roofs were heavily damaged. The water supply had been cut. In the town, even the buildings that had not had direct hits from the bombs burned for several days.

The Parignys lost everything. Their house was bombed and burned down. The personal possessions that I had not been able to fit into my little suitcase, such as my doll, burned. There were several victims, including the priest of St Hilaire, who baptized me and knew my story. Saint-Hilaire and its inhabitants paid a high price in the liberation of France. Although this little town was liberated on 2 August 1944, the battle raged on and on in the surrounding small towns and villages. The liberation of Lower Normandy, planned to take three weeks, took nearly three months.

The sound of the air raid sirens was very stressful. There was a background noise of the bombardments in the towns and countryside day and night. During the day it was the Americans and British and at night the British and Germans. We could even hear the bombs falling on the towns of Saint-Lô and Saint Malo! And then there was the battle of Mortain, fifteen kilometers from us. During operation Cobra, in July 1944 the troops advanced, and then fell back, kilometer by kilometer... Ground was taken and then lost..

Several times Daniel and I were in the field nearby when we heard the distant battle getting closer and the bullets flying near us. I don't know what kind of projectile it was but I felt the air move as it passed by my cheek. I was a little frightened, but Daniel was terrified. He was very much afraid every time there was an alert. It had a long-term impact on him. But over all we were happy, playing amidst the danger. The three of us (Michel was too grown up) played with other children, at being shopkeepers, keeping house, with dolls. The chickens and chicks were our dolls – my dolls in particular!

During those few months on the farm we were self-sufficient. We made our own bread, on Wednesday I think. The children congregated around the very fine stone oven situated outside the house. The warm crusty bread that came out of that wood-burning oven, spread with butter, was delicious! But needless to say – by the following Tuesday the bread was hard!

There were few men, either discharged from the army or in hiding to avoid being sent as forced labor to Germany. But most were in Germany in the "Obligatory Work Service", and they were called "STOs". Nothing was mechanized. The few remaining combine-harvesters no longer functioned. The harvest was gathered around 14 July, the French national holiday. It was exhausting work. The men harvested the wheat: it was cut and laid on its side. Then we, the women and children, struck it with a "flail", a stick resembling a broom handle on the end of which was a chain and attached to that was a small stick. You beat hard on the ground to separate the grains from their husks. We dried the hay in haystacks. Other children were on the side of the field, by the horse and carts. We helped to stack the hay gathered by the adults and then we were allowed to climb on the carts when they were filled up, and we travelled back to the farm on top of the hay. There we put the hay in the barn, and our great reward was to jump and slide on it. Daniel and I were the best at it! It was great fun, heavenly with lots of giggles!

We were in a hamlet near St. Brice. We went there for mass, on the cart pulled by the white mare. Wearing straw hats, we all squeezed onto the cart. We travelled down a lane that was just the width of the cart… The wheels caught in the ruts that were sometimes deep, sometimes rocky, but never smooth. Tree branches whisked off our hats and we laughed hobbling along!

On the farm personal hygiene was limited as we washed at sinks outside. I had furunculosis, very deep boils caused by a Staphylococcus infection. They were filled with pus and had to be lanced. I still have the scars on my body. Claudine and I also had scabies. It was between the fingers. It itched dreadfully. The only remedy at the time was to scrub with a scrubbing brush and black soap.

The countryside was very hilly. The farm was on one deep slope of the hill. One night I went out in the dark to go to the toilet. In front of me was a branch and on it an owl. And on the other side of the valley was a farm on fire, with its great beams in flames. The Germans had dropped a shell or a bomb on it.

There was a constant battle between planes. The allies had disembarked and were advancing. There were fierce battles between Saint-Hilaire-du-Harcourt and Mortain, which was retaken seven times.

Once again using his valuable experience of the First World War, M. Parigny had dug a trench behind the farm. And every night we went down into the trench (I've had rheumatism in my knees ever since!); it was like a tomb, and the top was covered with bundles of firewood. There were lots of glowworms, the only light except that of the moon.

The land and air battles to liberate Normandy lasted three months. We children recognized the airplanes by their sound: the B17s or American B24s flew in formations of six, twelve or more. They flew by day and carried out "carpet" bombing, releasing thousands of bombs. To hit a target such as a bridge or a munitions depot they wiped out whole neighborhoods or small towns. They made a continuous sound: "Voooooooooooooooon"! They dropped the bombs through clouds and that was frightening: you just heard the noise coming nearer. We didn't know where the bombs were dropped. It was these flying fortresses that frightened me the most.

The British on the other hand dived and aimed at a particular target: "VaaaaAAAAAnn, boom, VaaaaAAAAAnn, boom". They were in smaller squadrons than the bombers - fighter planes which literally picked out their targets as birds of prey do. They often attacked bridges.

As for the Germans, they had a very strange kind of fuel - they were short of everything, and their engines made a staccato irregular noise: "vuo vuonvuonvuonvuon". These were the most dangerous because they attacked civilian targets and farms as well as anti aircraft guns and fields where gasoline was stored. The bomber planes flew mostly at night and the fighter aircraft during the day. They dropped stick bombs. In addition to military installations, there were the Department of Civil Aviation and anti-aircraft guns; these guns fired on the planes in a spirit of destruction and revenge … in desperation! The more the allies advanced, the more the Germans came back to bomb the farms.

They were attacking everywhere, their bombs destroying everything. A chain of a dozen bombs not only took the roof off our farmhouse, but made great holes in the ground all around. Claudine and I slept in the kitchen, in a bed next to the fireplace. The bombing didn't wake me, even though when I woke I found the roof was almost blown off! Everyone was amazed that I didn't hear a thing!

The following day a German fighter plane near by was shot down. There was a knock on the door and it was the pilot and co-pilot of the plane on the doorstep, armed. We were all in the kitchen. M. Parigny opened the door and spoke to them. They asked for water, explained that they had been shot down, and asked what was the noise coming from the roads. M. Parigny explained that it was the allies on the roads. This the pilots didn't know and had difficulty believing! They opened their map of the region on the table to find out where they were.

After they had gone M. Parigny said: "they won't get far, they'll be arrested soon".

It was strictly forbidden to own a radio set under the Nazi regime. In any event they had all been requisitioned and M. Parigny had had to surrender his. However, after the appeal of Charles de Gaulle on 18 June 1940, the local group of resistants to the Nazi and Vichy régimes made "galena" radios and M. Parigny and Michel made their own. They were thus able to listen to the BBC's "Frenchmen talking to Frenchmen" a clandestine, coded program broadcast from

London. This was strictly forbidden and punishable by deportation. But M. Parigny was a man of courage.

With some of the other children we twice went to watch from of the main roads where the allied troops were passing. It was not far from the farm but was a bit of a walk. There was an old legend that said that a peasant had buried a treasure of gold crowns somewhere. So we had a double motivation: find this mythical treasure and meet up with some of those open-sided American trucks. The Americans, when they saw us, threw us candies, chocolates, chewing gum and little high-energy cookies that were much nicer than the ones handed out at school!

At the end of the summer we all went back to St. Hilaire to temporary housing. A few months after the liberation of Paris in August 1944, an organization called the European Service to find deported and displaced Jews (SER) began their work of helping families to find their family members and be reunited. I don't know how contact was made, but uncle Paul came to get me and took me back to Paris in December 1944. We were reunited with my grandmother at the shelter on the rue des Rosiers.

Normandy, those were happy years in spite of the fear, in spite of everything. I was in a world of children. I knew it wouldn't last but I enjoyed it nonetheless. I knew there were risks, so I knew I had to be obedient while I was there. I very much enjoyed being in a family. It was calming for me to be accepted and nurtured... My mother was somewhere, I would find her. I was waiting to see her again, and to see my grandmother. My dear mother had promised.

I went back on holiday at least twice to see the Parignys. I was very happy to discover again "my" Normandy. The family still lived in temporary housing, as their house had not yet been rebuilt. I went cycling again along those roads with the other children, but not as far as the village of Vérolay. I took lots of photos. I didn't yet know that I was about to leave France. My uncle Paul had mentioned it, but it was very difficult to obtain papers and we thought it wouldn't come to anything.

After a few more visits, I stayed in contact with the family until 1973, the year in which my grandmother and M. Parigny died.

XII - Paris (1945 – 1947)

I came back to Paris in December 1944 to 4 bis rue des Rosiers. The building in which we stayed had formerly been the headquarters of the ORT (Organization, Reconstruction, Travail), a philanthropic network of Jewish trade schools. It was a place where refugees came seeking family members, and where families were reunited. Not just foreign refugees, but also French families. Grandmother was there to greet me. I hadn't seen her for two years. She didn't know what my life had been. I was very disoriented in this big building, so different from the place I had just come from. On the famous rue des Rosiers, right in the middle of the Jewish quarter, with its dark, grey buildings. It was yet another complete break. Once again I had to adjust to something, somewhere new. It was another change of place, but it also felt like a step backwards. And it wasn't a homecoming! In Paris you could feel the war, whereas I had been living the life of innocence in Normandy despite the bombing. Even if there was no longer danger, I didn't feel any joy... Although I'm not sure that I felt anything at all at that time, during that period.

I was focused on the return of my mother. I was waiting for my mother. Grandmother and uncle Paul showed her photo to everyone. I showed her photo to everyone. To every deportee who had been sent to Auschwitz and had came to ORT from the hotel Lutecia to find his or her family, we showed my mother's photo. No one had seen her, but I persevered; I had only one thought, only one hope: to see her again.

Each one of us came out of their respective hiding place: grandmother from Vanves, my uncle Paul from the South

West and me from Normandy. Perhaps the fact that they were both there gave me a sense of injustice. Perhaps that is how it seems to me now as an adult. Anyway, they were a secondary priority in comparison to my mother. Paul was quick tempered but affectionate. In the rue des Rosiers when grandmother told him that my mother had been deported to a concentration camp, he burst into tears. I can still see him now.

I think that in my suitcase I had everything I owned in the world: a black overcoat, a dress, a pair of underwear, a pair of shoes and some spare socks, that was all. In any event, with the war shortages, and since children grow so fast, no one could afford many spare clothes. You could buy clothes on the black market, but that was expensive. Most children had a weekday dress and a Sunday dress. When going to school, children wore an apron over it.

Grandmother still had her few personal possessions that she had had at the beginning of the war. She was very thin, uncle Paul as well. I was of normal height and weight. I had never seen grandmother like that. Not that she had lacked food, but she had had many worries. She had bunions on her feet and her shoes were like great clogs on the end of her thin legs.

We - the non-deported Jews who had survived the genocide - took our meals in the great dining room on the ground floor along with those who had come back from the concentration camps. The deportees were in the Hotel Lutecia, but some of them, whose health was good enough, could rejoin their families in the rue des Rosiers, until they found their own accommodation. All that was temporary. I can still see the "residents" sitting at the tables in this refectory. There, one afternoon, I saw a man enter. He had hardly come in when several men stood up, and one in particular leapt on him and showered him with punches. He was a "Capo". Capos were those who - often recruited from among the most violent common criminals - kept guard over the prisoners in the concentration camps. This must have been a Jewish Capo, a Jew recruited by the Nazis to mistreat the other Jews. He too had come to find his family.

We slept in large dormitories on the first floor. They were former workshops. Men and women were separated. I slept next to my grandmother; we stretched pieces of fabric over strings to make a kind of screen, to try and have a little private space to dress and undress. I had just had my twelfth birthday and was just at the start of adolescence. I had the impression of being unclean: there was just a small washbasin. We went to the municipal baths.

I remember an old Polish woman who spoke to grandmother in Yiddish. My grandmother didn't understand her and she got angry, verbally attacking my grandmother, saying that we were not Jews if we didn't speak Yiddish. After what we had been through because we were Jewish, it was outrageous.

My German was rusty, disjointed. I understood everything, but had lost the fluency of expression. I tripped over words, and remembering vocabulary took me several seconds. Of course it came back very fast, after a month or so, as I spoke only German with my family.

We stayed in rue des Rosiers until May or June 1945. I remember the first of May when it snowed. I watched the snowflakes falling through the windowpanes. We were very cold.

I went to the Lycée Victor Hugo, on rue de Sévigny, where I finished the 1945 school year. Grandmother and I went to live in a hotel on rue du Parc Royal. My uncle Paul rented a room on rue de Malte in the 11th arrondissement.

During and immediately after the war, vermin were abundant. In the hotel, the fleas and bed bugs were climbing up the walls and biting us in the night. At school many children had fleas and lice. The nits or lice eggs stuck to my very black hair and were very visible! Grandmother had to buy a special comb and I went to a hairdresser next to the hotel to have my hair cut short. We had to constantly rinse the hair with vinegar, as the lice were tenacious and the children kept re-infecting each other.

There were kitchen facilities in the hotel room, a gas hot plate and a small table. The soap was very bad quality and though we washed ourselves, personal hygiene was very difficult. There were filthy toilets on the landing. We had no special products during and after the war to keep things clean.

We continued our search to find my mother; several search committees and services, national and international, were created after the war. Among these was the S.E.R to which we wrote. The reply arrived on 30 October 1945. We were already living on rue d'Ulm. The letter informed us that my mother had been deported on 29 July 1942 from Drancy to Auschwitz and that her name had not been found on any list of those liberated from the camps. The Auschwitz concentration camp had been liberated on 27 January 1945.

From the moment we knew that my mother was not on that list, I began to dream about what had happened to her.

For a long time, and still today, even though this hope has faded, I felt that one day I would see my mother again. That she was somewhere in those vast expanses to the East, resembling the Russian steppes.... Why Russia, I have no idea! For a long time I dreamt of setting out to look for her. All alone I crossed a field, which was furrowed with blood. The dream was in color – the blood I saw was red.

Rue du Parc royal was a narrow street. Our hotel was across the street of an old detached elegant mansion. My window was open and I was looking out. There was an American soldier at the window opposite. He was showing me an orange as if he wanted me to have it. I accepted. He threw it across the road and it fell into my room. It was my first orange. I don't even remember what it tasted like. I read several decades later that General J.C.H. Lee, the commander of the forces that liberated Paris, had been criticized for distributing the oranges that had arrived from North Africa to the troops in the capital instead of those at the front[25]. I was happy to benefit from that!

Paul had succeeded in obtaining a job as a salesman in leather goods. He had acquired a bicycle. I knew how to ride it and enjoyed it. I borrowed it from him to do a little tour of the neighborhood. Opposite the Place Payenne I managed to crash into one of the very rare cars on the streets of Paris at that time. The front wheel was buckled. I fell on the ground, but I was mainly frightened to death of going home and telling Uncle Paul that I had damaged his bike, which was vital to him earning his living. He was a generous man, but he was furious. I would never use his bicycle again.

We stayed in this neighborhood until the end of the school year, and then my uncle started actively looking for an apartment in the neighborhood he had lived in before the war.

We moved into 38, rue d'Ulm. It was a small apartment on the ground floor, giving onto the courtyard. This was partially paved. At the end on the right was a small stone hut and on the left, in front of our windows, was a large jardinière bordered with stones. The first thing my uncle did was to buy some radish seeds and sow them. He adored radishes! A cat and her kittens lived in the hut. Bliss for me!

Several charity events were organized right after the war for the survivors. I seem to remember that for one Jewish religious festival we were invited to a concert hall, perhaps at the Champs Elysées theater. There was a show for the children and then a distribution of gift packages. On that day I received a gift package that contained a magnificent pair of shoes. They came from the Quakers in the United States. They were caramel color, with leather laces and thick crepe soles: after my clogs and shoes with wooden soles, these shoes were a blessing, the ultimate! They were a superb

---

[25] A Genius of war, Carlo D'Este, Harper Collins, 1995.

present, I was so grateful to the little American girl who had bequeathed them to me. After the war all the talk was of reconstruction, the Marshall Plan… But we had nothing, so oranges, sweets, shoes, everything concrete, tangible was just wonderful.

The rue d'Ulm apartment was gradually furnished and decorated, notably with the contents of the five crates that had been packed and stored in Luxembourg, and which arrived on September 9, 1946. A friend, Mme Didong had carefully stored all the crates that my mother had entrusted to her. One contained the large portrait of my mother reading. So it had survived the war! It was a most precious possession that had survived.

I was accepted at the Lycée Fenelon in the fifth arrondissement. As it had been requisitioned during the war and was now being renovated, the class was housed for six months in the boys' school, the Lycée Montaigne on rue Auguste Comte. I chose the fifth grade in sciences: math, sciences and modern languages. Uncle Paul discouraged me from taking Latin and Greek, which he thought were pointless. Also, I hadn't done any Latin in Normandy nor during the short period of sixth grade at the Lycée Victor Hugo. I had to work hard to be able to keep my place in fifth grade at the Lycée Fénelon, where there were some really bright students. At home I had made myself a desk from the wooden crates that had come from Luxembourg, plus a little lamp. I often studied late into the evening. Then my uncle's voice would be raised, ordering me to turn out the light "you already know too much!" What a lack of understanding of my situation!

On the way home from school at midday, I was asked to do a little shopping in rue St Jacques, at the bakery and the dairy. I was incapable of reaching home without having broken off and eaten the end of the fresh baguette even though I was scolded when I arrived! I remember also the group of boys who gathered at the Art Deco school on rue d'Ulm, almost opposite our house. When I saw them, I didn't want to walk past them – I was afraid of their teasing! I waited for them to disperse. The schools were not integrated and I was very intimidated by boys. In fact the only ones I knew were my friend Fabienne's brothers and the Parigny sons.

The stone wall of the courtyard was shared by a convent, which is no longer there. I could hear the nuns singing and reciting their prayers as they walked. There was a gentle feel to life in the neighborhood of the rue d'Ulm. I tried to live in a dream, rather than in sorrow. I thought that my mother would have liked to live in that place. I felt her close to me.

At the end of 1945 uncle Martin came to visit. It was a disastrous time for me. But it was also moving, as the two brothers greeted each other like two adolescents. It was the first time they had seen each other since before the beginning of the war. Grandmother told him what had been my mother's fate. He was very sad, but did not cry. Uncle Paul then told him what had happened to us during the war. Speaking of me, Paul said, "She too has suffered as we all have". To which Martin replied "that is nothing in comparison to her mother". That cut me like a dagger. I, who already felt guilty so easily! What I had been through – had it so little importance? I was hurt and angered by his reaction. I had never been very fond of him; this sealed it.

In fact, until I heard this conversation, I had not realized that I had suffered. His words brought to the surface something that until then had not been there. Reflecting on this today I think that he projected on to me what he reproached of himself. My mother, who often had helped him in the past, had written to Martin begging him to help her, but he had been unable to do so. I had survived and he resented me for it.

I have another memory of his short stay. It was still a time of shortages and everything was rationed. Uncle Paul hoarded everything. Uncle Martin wanted an aspirin. Paul opened a cupboard and there were pills on one of the shelves and nails and bits of string on the door. He gave one of the pills to his brother who exclaimed, half joking, half serious "how do you know what you're giving out?"

The adolescent years spent at the Lycée Fénelon were most essential in my psychological, spiritual and social development. These post war years in Paris shaped my world outlook. The war years had matured our generation beyond our age. I met some extraordinary girls there, and made adolescent friendships, which if we were to meet again today, would surely still be fresh. My great friend at that time was Fabienne Guillermont. She lived at 27 Boulevard St. Michel and was a member of the French Scouts. She was a bright student and excellent at math, which earned her my great admiration (I liked math but I had to work hard at it). She came from a bourgeois background; her father was an engineer. Her elder brother was charming; he must have been about 17. She also had a younger brother and a younger sister. I went there for tea, or she came to my house. Her parents were very nice, but they didn't allow us to jump on the beds! Whereas, in the rue d'Ulm there was an alcove and if we closed the curtains we could transform the bed into a stage. We put on plays when grandmother and uncle Paul were out. Often we were three or four friends who lived close by.

I joined the same scouting group – "les Eclaireuses neutres de France" - in part made up of girls from my class. Scouting suited my outlook on life. Nature, geology and animals attracted me. Scouting offered practical tasks: manual activities, I made benches, tables, and lamps.... Socializing, pushing ones limits, doing good deeds, and helping one another: I liked doing these tasks and they helped me to overcome my adolescent shyness.

In addition, there were many children of Sorbonne professors at the Lycée Fenelon, and there were groups of all ages of teenagers. Discussions really took off. They ranged from life and death issues to beliefs and religion. Without any attempt to convert, each person expressed what he or she believed in. I welcomed discussions about God, and saw that what would suit me best would be to not believe in God or in any dogma.

We tried also to integrate the less well-off girls, who lived in the neighborhood dilapidated housing. On Sundays I went to meet up with a girl on the rue Mouffetard, a very nice, petite brunette. I remember this steep street, full of women street sellers, with their wheelbarrows. They wore plaited straw shoes with wooden soles and lined with sheepskin to keep them warm. Some of them didn't have permits and when they saw the police coming they gave a shrill whistle to warn all the others. They hid in passages and alleys to avoid paying taxes.

I had a difficult adolescence at home. Uncle Paul had very fixed ideas about what a girl from a respectable family should be. She should not be a girl scout. He talked of the girls that he saw on city buses, with their backpacks, legs apart, not at all ladylike. Whereas for me the scouting movement was my happiness, my family, I felt understood there. Yet it was thanks to uncle Paul that I loved nature, he drew very well and through his painter's eyes made me discover the beauty of a tree and the multiple colors of its bark. He was opposed to my going to scout camp. I think that was the only time while we were in France that I got down on my knees to beg him. He gave in. The first camp was on the grounds of a chateau in the Creuse and the second at Saint Mards d'Ouilly in Normandy. I was also able to go to the great Scout Jamboree in 1947, which was the first post war meeting and was held in Moisson, France. The Nazis forbade the movement. I continued to be a scout until the age of 19.

The 1946 school year was spent in the Lycée's main building on 47, rue de l'Eperon near Boulevard St Germain.

It was during that same year that I received a letter from a French Canadian family in Montréal. They were responding to a drive initiated by one of their journalists to help French war orphans. I seemed to qualify. Thus started a correspondence with Mme Massicotte and her daughter Hélène who was of the same age as I. They sent not only letters but also packages with much needed food and clothing. My exchange of letters with Hélène lasted well into adulthood.

I enjoyed this period not only because of my friends, but also because of the new subjects I was studying at the lycée. I don't think I missed a single lesson during the entire time there. I had to be really ill. I was like a sponge, I had a thirst for knowledge, I wanted to know how things worked. I loved school; one radiant young woman, a natural sciences teacher, awoke my interest in geology - the structure of rocks in particular, and in science and everything connected. But to be a geologist, what I dreamed of being, was ridiculous and certainly not a job for a woman, according to my uncle.

Uncle Paul had to support us financially. At the beginning he earned a meager salary and we had to start again from zero – we did not own a single thing beyond some clothing. As time went by, uncle Paul began to make a good living.

I took bus number 38 near the Panthéon to get to rue de l'Eperon and he gave me the bus fare. Since I had received no pocket money, if I wanted to buy myself something, I had to walk 45 minutes from rue d'Ulm to rue de l'Eperon. This is how I discovered a second hand bookshop on rue Claude Bernard. I bought some books from the "Green library", a collection of books for adolescents. I still have some of them. Behind Place St. Michel, on Place St. André des Arts, there was a shop that sold rock samples and geologists' instruments. It is from that shop that I built up my collection of rocks, the ones I didn't find on my walks in the outskirts of Paris. Those little rocks were my jewels…

The three of us resumed our traditional roles. Grandmother the mother, uncle Paul the father and I was the child. I was an adolescent and I had my own ideas, but they had different ones, more conservative. On Sunday afternoons we went to visit some elderly friends and I was bored stiff. To greet them, I shook their hand and curtsied. I had learnt the curtsy in church!

Uncle Paul introduced me to the opera, buying tickets for "Mignon" by Ambroise Thomas. We had box seats and I enjoyed it enormously. But he had lived for a year in Milan and had gone to the opera at every opportunity – he had seen everything. He fell asleep and started to snore! I tapped him gently to wake him up: "uncle Paul, uncle Paul"!

He had girlfriends. He was a seducer but not a Don Juan. He liked pretty women, but one at a time! I met three of them. On July 14, 1946, the French national holiday, we were sitting on the terrace of a café on the boulevard St. Germain with one of these girlfriends. Music was playing and people were dancing in the street. My uncle was an excellent ballroom dancer. He invited me to dance, teaching me the steps - under the jealous eye of his girlfriend. She had come to be with him and found herself sitting at a table watching us dance!

I remember another of my uncle's girlfriends, Régine. She had invited the three of us to tea at her house. She lived in an apartment a little like that of the miliner, decorated throughout in white satin. She was a communist; my uncle was somewhat to the right. The discussion went back and forth: she was living in this luxurious apartment while defending values that were in stark contrast. She said several times that the apartment didn't belong to her, that she rented it. She also came to dinner to our apartment and for the occasion I painted my nails with colorless nail polish. When she saw the nail polish she started a diatribe about bourgeois customs. And she was living in white satin!

Uncle Paul also bought me a membership to a swimming pool in the Latin Quarter, where I learned to swim. He seemed to feel obliged to spend his free time with grandmother and I; he laughed and said that he was fulfilling his family duty. On Sunday afternoons he took us to the Luxembourg Gardens and from time to time we took the Sceaux railway line to the beautiful Parc de Sceaux.

Uncle Paul bought me my first new clothes. We went to the rue de Rivoli and I bought a dress, a coat and a lovely raffia handbag, which could be worn across the shoulder. He had good taste but he let me choose. He also bought me my first fountain pen – a big event. The pen shop was on the Boulevard St Michel, near rue Soufflot, on the left side descending the street. It was a revolution, because we normally wrote with a dip pen with its ink well. I was very proud of this fountain pen and kept it a long time.

Quite early on he bought a car, a black Citroen 11, which we used to go on short holidays. One particularly memorable trip was to St-Germain-en-Laye where we spent the Easter holidays in a guesthouse. Hans Isenberg, my uncle's very close friend, whom he had tracked down, came to St Germain with his wife Suzanne. The latter was a French woman who had hidden him during the war. She was not good looking and was demanding. My uncle felt very sorry for Hans for having married such a disagreeable woman.

At the hotel, while the adults were resting on deck chairs, I came across a tiny kitten that had an eye infection. I took care of it, and gave it eye baths of warm water. Then I thought I'd take it back to Paris, I knew uncle Paul was against it, so I simply put it in my bag and we all got in the car. Unfortunately for me and for the cat, it started to meow. I had to let it go.

After the war my uncle tried to get in touch with my father and his family, who were living in Rio. As I mentioned, my mother's brothers strongly disliked my father and held him responsible for a lot of things, including, no doubt, the death of my mother. Uncle Paul wrote letters to him in which he demanded money, saying that my father had not done his duty, and that he, Paul, was taking care of me. He called his brother-in-law Monsieur Deichmann, never Kurt.

On the other side, my family in Brazil was trying to make contact with my mother. The first letter, dated 10 October 1942, seven weeks after her death, was addressed to my mother through the intermediary of a Swiss company that my uncle Erich worked with. Uncle Erich sent 100 Swiss francs to my mother. Later a letter came through the Red Cross addressed to my mother at rue Caffarelli and dated 13 April 1944. This letter was sent via Geneva and arrived in Paris in November 1944. My uncle Paul must have received it in the months that followed for he wrote back early in 1945 to ask for money. The Red Cross received the reply on 10 May 1945! This shows how difficult it was to exchange correspondence during and immediately after the war.

It was only in 2000, after the death of my father, that I first heard of this correspondence. My Brazilian cousins gave the letters to me. I also learned later from my aunt Gerty, that my paternal grandfather in Brazil always said of me "We will find her".

The "Aufbau" ("Construction"), a German newspaper, was a very important means of communication for the German-speaking Jewish community the world over. This newspaper, founded in 1934, became one of the most important anti-Nazi newspapers in the German language. Hannah Arendt, Albert Einstein, Thomas Mann and Stefan Zweig were among its contributors. I remember seeing copies at home from December 1944 onwards. Also, it was from this year on that many lists of survivors began to be published. The newspaper also published information about families, at their request. It was in this way that I learned of the death of my paternal grandmother in Rio.

One afternoon in July 1946, grandmother, my uncle and I went to the famous Dalloyau ice cream shop on rue de Médicis. There I met my Brazilian aunt Germaine, nicknamed Gerty and my little cousin Myriam, who was ten years younger than me, who were on a trip to Europe. There was a lively conversation between the adults, but I was not listening. It was afterwards that I found out that they had come to take me with them to Brazil. Grandmother was vigorously opposed to it saying "I have lost my daughter; she entrusted her daughter to me, and while I am alive she will stay with me". So I didn't go to Brazil and I am extremely grateful.

In the meantime, uncle Paul had restarted the process for emigration to the United States, first started before the war. I had absolutely no idea what was about to happen to me. He hesitated to go, and then he thought he would have a very much better life over there. He also wanted to find a former flame of his, Hannelore Weil, who had immigrated to New York before the war.

The papers for emigration to America were ready. In the spring we got our "affidavit"; my uncle booked our passage. In 1947 there were few ways of travelling and one was to take a military convoy boat that had been converted back into a passengers ship. Ocean liners were no doubt still requisitioned by the government.

Heavy hearted I left France on 31 August 1947 with grandmother and uncle Paul for a short stay in London with uncle Martin. The journey from Paris to London was nonetheless magnificent: we took "La Flèche d'Or", the luxury boat train that went from Paris to Calais. At Calais, a boat took us to Dover, and from there an English train, the "Golden Arrow" took us to London. I have fabulous memories of that journey. I remember the white cliffs of Etretat shining in the afternoon sunlight. They were my last images of my sweet France.

I could not possibly imagine what awaited me on the other side of the Atlantic.

XIV - Sailing to New York...and back to France (September 1947 – December 1953)

It was on a late summer's day, Thursday 12 September 1947, that we embarked for America on the "SS Marine Jumper". The boat had been one of a fleet of troop transport ships during the Second World War. It could accommodate more than 6000 men. My uncle would have preferred a liner, but the waiting list was too long. In order to immigrate to the United States I had a "refugee" passport 19 pages long, many letters and documents attesting to my life's journey thus far.

The interior layout of the boat had not changed since the war. We slept in dormitories with rows of triple bunk beds. There were also single cabins for former officers. I think that grandmother and uncle Paul had a room of their own. In the dining rooms were rows of long tables. They had small wooden edges to stop the plates and glasses from falling off with the pitching of the boat. I was dreadfully seasick. Those boats were not as stable as the big liners. I stayed lying down for three days and then I got up and spent all my time on the bridge. The crossing took ten days. By staying on the bridge, I could follow with my eyes the movement of the boat – and its passengers! There were a lot of young people on board. I befriended one girl, a French student and a Guatemalan scout who was returning home from the "Jamboree" in Moisson. We recognized each other easily because it was the custom to wear a small scout badge or brooch for the girls, either on a collar or on the lapel. We were a large crowd of French people on board and we had a big party.

We arrived in New York on 22 September 1947, after passing through immigration controls on Ellis Island, a small island behind the Statue of Liberty, of which I took a photo! Disembarkation was complicated, because the mayor of New York, Fiorello LaGuardia had just died and the city was in mourning. The Dockers were not unloading the ships that day, and we had to stay on board for an extra night!

Aunt Ida was waiting for us on the dockside. But before disembarking, my uncle Paul warned me strongly against talking to any strangers. He also told me that a representative of my father's family might be on the dockside.

My private diary more or less stops at that date. Once again I had been completely uprooted and was crying almost every day.

Apart from Léon Bock, grandmother's oldest brother who had immigrated to the United States at the beginning of the twentieth century and of whom the family had had absolutely no news, four of my grandmother's brothers and sisters escaped the Nazi régime between 1939 and 1940. There were Jules, Karl, and his wife Erna, Theodor and Ida. Like all impoverished political immigrants they had to earn a living. Aunt Ida spoke English very well and easily found an administrative post. The brothers and Erna, who couldn't find jobs in commerce, became manual or restaurant workers. I never met my uncles Karl and Theodor who both died of cancer a few years after they immigrated. Theodor contracted a type of cancer directly linked to his work using radium paint. When she arrived in New York, grandmother and I stayed with Aunt Erna for several weeks. She worked in a tailor's workshop; it was very exhausting piecework with little pay. She was an imposing woman and made my poor grandmother's life very difficult.

My uncle Paul, who's English was very good, quickly found a job as a salesman. He rented several rooms in an apartment on Broadway. Once again it was temporary. When our trunks and my mother's crates arrived it was to this apartment that they were delivered. The latter were never unpacked – there was not enough space. When I unpacked my own possessions, in particular my rock collection, each one wrapped separately, my uncle made a scene. He accused me of already costing a lot to feed and clothe, without adding the cost of transporting useless items. I was a burden to him; he often said so when he was angry. I was overcome with grief by his words. In addition I was totally uprooted in a new country, in a new culture and in a strange town that I didn't like. And he was taking me further away from France and from my past.

The next day, in despair, I took my precious rocks and my souvenirs and threw them into the incinerator. There were incinerators on the landing of each floor. It was like a suicide – if I could have disappeared with my rocks I would have done so.

Another subject of dispute between my uncle and I was my schooling. I would love to have gone to the Lycée Français of New York, a French school, but it was out of the question. I had to adapt to American society he told me, and sent me to George Washington High School, which was free. It was way north of Manhattan and I went there by subway. It was a very large high school of about 3000 students. Henry Kissinger, who also lived in Washington Heights, had attended several years earlier. I had studied English as a second language for one year in Paris. My knowledge of German helped me enormously to pick it up quickly. I often stood in front of the bathroom mirror and pronounced "brown cow now" in order to exercise my facial muscles and help my pronunciation. It was the latter that was the most difficult. After six months or so, I could speak American. Once again, I just wanted to be like the other students, even if deep inside I was thousands of miles away. The culture of American girls of my age was extremely different to that of Europeans: they wore make up, and talked of nothing but boys and cars. I made friends mostly with the Europeans. My first group of friends was a group of white Russians, with whom I played tennis. But they were so totally disorganized that I distanced myself from them. I had lost everything that I loved, and my future seemed bleak. Once again I had to mourn a part of myself.

The northerly winds of uptown Manhattan on Riverside Drive were freezing. You had to cover your face. I had sinusitis and my first migraines. From the rue d'Ulm to Washington Heights, the German Jewish quarter of New York, the change was so heartrending that I cried for months; from one world to another at the age of fourteen and a half ... to be uprooted like that was unbearable to me.

Meanwhile my uncle had found a large, fine apartment at the intersection of 990 Riverbank Drive and 161st Street, and we all lived there together. Grandmother, Paul - his wife came later, on their marriage in 1951 - and me, and also my great aunts, Ida and Friedl, who arrived from the Theresienstadt concentration camp in 1948, and my uncle Jules and his wife Cilli. I lived there until my departure for France after my marriage at the end of 1953, and then again when we returned as a family from 1955 to 1957.

There was a large corridor like a bowling alley. The seven rooms were in a line, except for the bathroom, a maid's room, and the kitchen, which looked out the back. The other rooms looked out onto the Hudson, the park and tennis courts, lawns that curved upwards over the slope. My bedroom was near the crossroads and my grandmother's, the finest room, was right on the intersection. In fact she said later: "I don't want to go on holiday it is so beautiful here". We could see New Jersey and the George Washington Bridge. Very little traffic passed on Riverside Drive at that time. It was still a modern apartment and we occupied every room: the living room I remember had folding French doors. It also contained a sofa bed that Cilli and Jules folded up every day.

The building was six floors high and was built in 1921 in a neighborhood that was very fashionable before the Second World War. With all the penniless European refugees it became less so, and then that group of people left at the end of the 1950s. It later became a Black and Puerto Rican neighborhood, a place with gangs. Recently the building and the whole neighborhood have been completely renovated to their former splendor.

There was a smaller apartment on our floor. A couple of single Jewish women lived there, friends of my Aunt Ida, who had arrived before the war and were widows for the most part. Mrs. Hess was a singing teacher who accompanied herself on the piano, then there was Mrs. Jonas, and a lodger who we nicknamed the monk. He was a bachelor. To earn some pocket money I sewed curtains for Mrs. Hess and did housework for this man. To thank me, he gave me a magnificent old alarm clock that showed the phases of the moon. My cultural and musical development continued in New York. Mrs. Hess was a great music lover and I went with her to public rehearsals. Thus I attended my first great concert, a rehearsal: Bruno Walter conducting the New York Philharmonic Orchestra playing Schubert's Unfinished Symphony. The first time I went to Carnegie Hall was to see Aida from a seat in the high gallery. I had a bird's eye view of Aida's bosom: such a fine voice in such a large body!

There was a French library downtown, near the French Lycée, a long way from where I lived. That summer I was 16 years old, and I read classic after classic: Zola, Balzac, Maupassant, and Dostoyevsky. I have always been an avid reader. Little by little I created a new world for myself.

In Paris, before leaving, I had been given the name of a Girl Scout troop attached to the Lycée Français. I very soon joined this group and from that moment on all my free time and my extracurricular activities took place at the Lycée. It was my lifeline. All my friends were either French by birth or like me, French by adoption. The majority of students had come to New York to be safe from Nazism or the Vichy régime.

A new scout group was created at the Lycée in 1946. Three former Scouts from France created it: Robert Kaminker, Robert Boas and Boris Gorlin, all of different religions and from different branches of the Scouting movement, which made for a very ecumenical group. It was composed of the children of French people, or people who had emigrated from France and who found themselves in New York. We were a non-denominational troop but our scouting was "à la française", our uniforms and structure were French, and above all we had not adopted the material comforts of the American scouts.

We were made up of people from all levels of society: from the high bourgeoisie to modest incomes, to the intellectuals. I was one of the very few in the troop who did not attend the Lycée Français but was totally into France. In our small nostalgic community we listened to Charles Trenet's songs especially "Douce France" ad nauseam... We discussed existentialism, the meaning of life, suicide. It was appropriate to the times. Some of us had had to face death.

We hosted French-speaking scout troops passing through New York, for example from Canada or Martinique. At one meeting I met Ambroise Lafortune, a Canadian priest who was very well known in his country. This opened my eyes considerably, this contact with Canada and the Caribbean. In New York, everyone mixed together; it was truly international, whereas in France the Scouts were either Catholic, Protestant, Jewish or non-denominational, my group in Paris the latter.

I continued to correspond with the Canadians for many years, with Père Ambroise but also with Louise Joubert, Gilles de Beauregard and Claire Dupond who were journalists or poets involved in the Québec independence movement in the sixties. The French Lycée, which was situated downtown, was our assembly point.

Aside from the scouts, I also continued to correspond with my other Canadian friend, Hélène Massicotte, well into the 1950's.

One of the French pupils who were scouts was Max Marest. He fell in love with me, but his feelings were not at all reciprocated! The poor boy came every day to George Washington High School. As I wasn't interested he got discouraged. I would have much preferred his brother Gérard who I went on street marches with me in New York.

At that time I also befriended Beate Friedman. She was born in Austria. Her parents had fled Nazism and were divorced. She was the same age as me, but came from a much more intellectual background. Her mother often welcomed me to their apartment. She had remarried to Louis Rougier the philosopher. Beate excelled at math, played the guitar and belonged to the scouts. Every time we came home from a scout camp, we passed the first night at her house, where we slept on the floor! Later I became a "senior" scout as well as a scout leader. I left that wonderful youth movement shortly before my marriage.

Fabienne Guillermont – from Paris – and I had corresponded for about two years, in 1948 and 1949. Then I became so homesick for France that I cut all contact with my former friends in Paris. It became unbearable; it only served to revive my feeling of loss.

I joined the French choir when I was about 17 or 18. There I met a boy, my first love. We were rehearsing Beethoven's Ninth symphony. I fell in love with him and had never felt that kind of strong feeling for a boy. He was 21 and looked down on me. He was working and was a scout. He was a "grown up" He took me to the cinema. And he gave me my first kiss. I saw him again at the dances and parties at the Lycée and we danced together. His name was Pierre Lair. He was the son of a chemical engineer who had come to work in New Jersey and had not wanted to go back to France.

First kiss, first heartbreak. We were to meet downtown, but he stood me up. I waited a long time for him; he never came. I arrived home sulky and fed up. My grandmother asked: what happened to you?" and I answered her rudely. My uncle slapped me: "you don't speak to your grandmother like that!" It was the last slap I received in my life.

The group also produced a performance of "Topaz", a play written by Pagnol, a French playright and author. I played a prostitute. The moment I was due to go on stage, I couldn't say a word! Fortunately there were understudies and my friend Alice Lorsy, who was a dancer at the Balanchine Ballet, took my place. Artistic life has always flourished in New York and as Europeans we were particularly spoilt: many great artists had fled there as refugees and others arrived straight after the end of the war. Thus I was able to see Louis Jouvet, a great French actor, perform and give a conference.

At 18, when I started university, I also made friends with some of the American students. Some were from Columbia and one, a medical student, came to the house to collect me and we went to a student party at his fraternity. At the party, he flirted with me, the students were getting drunk and the atmosphere became unacceptable to me. He was obsessed with the desire to sleep with me and showed me no respect. I got away from him and went home disgusted. I should add that at the time French women – and in the eyes of Americans I was French - had a reputation for being women of easy virtue.

I befriended poets and writers. Quite boring and stuffy. One of them was very nice and respecful towards me, writing poems and songs, but I wasn't ready. I left him in a taxi and never saw him again.

While in that milieu, I met a young woman called Stephanie Haïmov. She was a Czech refugee, very beautiful and kind. She was a nurse or medical doctor. Her ex-husband was a writer. She spoke French with a Slav accent, and rolled her "r"s. She was a friend of the biologist Julian Huxley who lived in Greenwich Village. We would go to his house – I remember the very young children of this couple, having to quietly listen to Bach! It was also with her that I went to my first jazz concerts. Gene Krupa playing drums fascinated me.

Soon after our arrival, my uncle changed his name. It is easy to legally change one's family name in the United States. My uncle called himself Caron instead of Aron and hoped in this way to avoid prejudice in the job market. For one should not imagine that there was no anti-Semitism in the United States. It was very strong, as were other forms of racism. Blacks travelled in the back of buses and subway train cars. New Yorkers frequently took holidays in the nearby Catskill Mountains. Some of these large guesthouses had big signs on the lawn saying "gentiles only". Thus we encountered anti-Semitism… on display. But America was sectarian and community oriented – so we were not overly offended. Being part of one community or another was a way of life and immigrants conformed to it. In any event they could live their lives without going to such tourist destinations for example. I immediately felt empathy for the Blacks that seemed to me to be even more disadvantaged and excluded than all the others.

Incidentally, it was when we immigrated to the United States that I was confronted with the issue of nationality. Not with the immigration authorities, not because of the fact that I was stateless – I had all the necessary papers proving that I was a refugee coming from Germany – but with ordinary Americans. When someone asked me what nationality I was, "stateless" was apparently not an adequate reply. They wanted to know if I was French, German or Jewish! When I started to explain, the reaction was always "well then, you are Jewish", which never failed to infuriate me. I never got used to that kind of thinking. I had always thought that the fact of being Jewish was not a nationality, but was a religion, or at most a historical fact. There existed a population and ethnic entity in a country in the Middle-East. 2000 years ago, these Jews dispersed around the world. They mostly migrated west. Even with the religious rituals and beliefs, they mingled with other populations. For 2000 years, Jews have mixed with other ethnic groups. But in the United States during the post war era, thinking went from the Middle Ages to Nazism, ignoring the philosophers of the Enlightenment! The Jewish question is one that still bothers me today[26]. According to Jewish Law, one remains Jewish, in terms of Jewish Identity even when one is no longer a Jew, in terms of Judaism. One is always a Jew. It was amazingly difficult to explain that one could be stateless, Jewish and atheist all at once! In particular in the fifties, in the middle of the Cold War, when being an atheist was tantamount to being a communist.

I finished High School in 1950 and enrolled at New York University. There again was another family drama. I chose to study Geology at Hunter College, a university for women. But my uncle was furious: "that is not a career for a woman. You draw well; you can be a designer or a secretary. I'm telling you, if you study Geology or another unsuitable subject, you will have to pay rent and contribute to your upkeep ". So I stopped and after a semester I signed up for night classes and found a secretarial job at Longines. I wrote cards to people to tell them their watches were ready. In any event, my uncle was fed up with feeding me, he told me so in no uncertain terms. The night classes included history, English, math… anything that didn't require laboratory work to be done during the day. But it was difficult at the time to manage both night courses and day job.

In 1952 I tried training as a nurse at the Bellevue Hospital, which was a public hospital. I boarded there and

---

[26] Retour sur la question juive, Élisabeth Roudinesco, Albin Michel, 2009.

followed practical and theory courses there for six months. I quickly realized it wasn't for me. It was above all the attitude of the doctors – both men and women – towards the nurses that was so disagreeable. Several rather humiliating incidents happened: a doctor who watched me lift the arms of a cardiac patient insulted me, saying that I would never amount to anything. I did not know the patient had a heart condition.

Thankfully, I met Adele Meggers, a quiet student of German origin, and she did become a nurse. We did something that was crazy for that era in America: we hitchhiked on the Highway from New York to Texas to go and visit the brother of a French friend. He was part of a group of young French pilot trainees at the Laredo airbase! We had some near-miss accidents and aggressions but a very kind truck driver gave us the money to finish the journey to Laredo on a Greyhound bus. In Laredo I got to fly: I co-piloted a light aircraft – a piper cub. At the end or our visit, they all contributed to buy us return tickets to New York by bus, a 72-hour journey!

I tried to contribute financially to family life ... I was able to buy my first dress (dark red cotton with small white squares) thanks to my time as an au pair with a WASP family who made me feel very welcome. They were originally English and lived in Massachusetts. With them I ate a very memorable oyster stew. I then worked as a waitress on Shelter Island, right at the end of Long Island in a small family guesthouse. We were six young waitresses, all students, and the guests were very pleasant. It seemed that I prepared a good hot chocolate, and one of the guests gave me a medal!

I also worked as the governess of a 12-year old boy who had broken his leg. Then I worked for the family of the famous toymaker Louis Marx. I looked after his youngest child in their country home outside New York. The mother was a trophy wife, an adorable and very beautiful ex -model.

During this time my uncle continued to apply for a pension for me from the French government. In 1946 he received a statement from the Ministry for Veterans and war victims (Ancients Combatants), certifying that I was listed as a French war victim. In 1953 he again wrote to the same ministry, applying for compensations. The reply was negative, the reason given: I no longer lived on French soil! The same thing for Germany: I hadn't lived there long enough.

After my experience in the world of work, I had a long discussion with my uncle, because I wanted to return to France. My homesickness was still as strong in spite of everything. With the money I had saved while I was with the Marx family, I wanted to pay for my trip. My uncle said "keep the money, don't go". But in January 1953 I set sail for France on the "Flandres" and I returned to New York in March of the same year on the "Ile de France".

I stayed in a hotel not far from the Louvre. I met up with my friends from America, in particular Eliane Graf, whose brother was a pilot in Laredo. He had a friend named Raymond Lamy who was in love with me. He wanted to get married but it wasn't very clear. I was discovering new horizons; I went skiing with him in Meribel-les-Allues. Above all I was elated to be in Paris...the morning's croissants cheered me up so much! But there was no way I could stay: I had no one in France and I was still a student.

On the boat journey home I met a certain Jacques Debossu. We danced together and then we wrote to each other, as he was in Denver on an airbase. He was charming, a good dancer and treated me with delicacy and respect, gentle I would say. He made up stories about his family, but that didn't matter: he was French! I went to visit him in Colorado. We went camping in Golden, an old gold mining town. He was fascinated by America, idealizing it as much as I adored France. He asked me to marry him before returning to France. He was very much in love with me. In despair I said yes. My family didn't object, they left me free to go ahead. Only uncle Paul said to me: "We don't know his family, I'd like to hire a private detective in France". I refused.

On the eve of the wedding I was crying in my room. My grandmother came to me and said, "if you want to Marion, we can cancel everything", to which I replied "no, I've come this far, I promised, it's too late".

We got married on September 30, 1953. We had two or three days' honeymoon in a hotel on Times Square. I was very modest and didn't want to undress.

He had to finish an Air Force assignment in France and I went back to my family until December. Then I traveled to France on my own and Jacques came to meet me at Le Havre. During my first pregnancy we lived in Reims. We then went to live in Laon, in the Aisne department, where my first son was born on November 11, 1954. Jacques' father had lost his job and also lost his pension. His parents lived with us until the father found a job in Bordeaux. We went to live with them for a few months before traveling back to America.

We returned to New York in November 1955. Jacques hadn't found work that he liked in France and thought that it would be different in America. As we disembarked from the liner "Liberté", we were met not only by our family but also by a journalist who took a photo of my son. The picture appeared on the front page of the New York World Telegram on 30 November 1955!

Initially, for me, the only good thing about returning to live in America was the feeling that the war was definitely behind us, in the past. I had since become used to this country and appreciated it. Nostalgia for France remained deep within me, in spite of everything.

There was not much physical body contact in my family. Although my mother kissed me before I went to bed, neither my grandmother nor my uncle did. It wasn't something that

Germans did, after the years of very early childhood. Whereas in Normandy, people kissed five times every time they met!

I must add that during all those years in New York my grandmother and I never talked about the war. Grandmother never recovered from the loss of her daughter, of her home and from being uprooted. She was entirely dependent on her two sons. She was not a sad person though; she was always on my side in my arguments with my uncle, and she knew how to laugh. At 67 it was difficult to adapt to life in the United States. In fact grandmother went back to Europe in 1956 to be with her other son, my uncle Martin in London. She died peacefully in 1973 in a retirement home at the age of 93. I loved her very much, but was never able to show her how much.

XIII - My life in America

From New York City we moved to California in August 1957. The time spent in California was a most important time in my life. I lived there for 13 years. My formative years were over and I was able to rebuild my life.

The 1960's were the years of awakening, enlightenment and political awareness. California is where the Free Speech movement was born. It spread across the whole country. It was the much regretted President Kennedy era.

I attended the University of California to finish my degree. I became politically active during the Vietnam War. My family had grown and I became the mother of four children, one of whom was handicapped. We lived in Riverside, a small university town in southeastern California, and though we had recurrent financial problems those were very happy years. To watch my children grow up was a joy and a discovery. I was able to take up my studies thanks to the ambiance of cooperation that existed on campus, where childcare was available. I found a part-time job at the University and we were able to live on campus for a while in student housing. There was great upheaval in society after the assassination of President Kennedy in November 1963, with the war in Vietnam and the invasion of Cambodia. I participated fully in this revolution - it was for my future, for our future. I had the impression that I was not a victim of my fate but that I could change things. It was intellectually stimulating to take part in the political life of "my" country. I became an American citizen in 1961, after so many years of statelessness. I was proud. I seemed to be able to envision the future.

The following decade was to be very different. After a brief time in Zurich in 1967 we returned to France. Jacques had found a good job and thought that it would please me too. But I was well integrated into life in California where I had lived thirteen years, and my past suddenly seemed a long time away! Nonetheless, we settled in Lyon in July 1970. I rekindled my enthusiasm for fighting for ecological causes, most notably against Superphénix, the nuclear power plant!

XIV - Reunion with my father

Several years after moving to California, I wanted to meet my father. I was living with my husband and my three eldest children, far away from my grandmother and uncle. I was 28 years old. I felt the need to see the mostly unknown other family that I came from. I wrote a long letter to my father, explaining what had happened to me and telling him that I would like to see him again. That I had no resentment, and I had no feeling of vengeance, I just wanted to know him. We had parted when I was four years old. Or rather he had left us then.

I never received a reply. I blamed the Brazilian postal service since I had obtained his address in Rio through a lawyer that uncle Paul had contacted. Meanwhile, in 1945, uncle Erich had written letters to the Red Cross from Brazil to find out whether I had survived. The family knew that my mother had died because uncle Paul had written to them.

Many years had passed. I returned to Europe in 1970. I started to work in Geneva in 1976 in an international organization, the World Health Organization (WHO). People of many nationalities worked there and I had a Brazilian friend. One day during a get-together at my house, I said to her "My paternal family lives in Brazil, in Rio but I've not succeeded in making contact with them". She replied straight away: "I'm going there at Christmas, give me their names." I gave all the information I had to this colleague; she went to Rio and contacted my aunt. Apparently she exploded with joy: "Give me her address. Tomorrow I will talk to her father". She phoned me, we talked in German, and she said, "Your father will call you tomorrow evening". It was right at the end of December 1980.

The next day I heard my father's moved voice on the other end of the line. I was surprised by the beautiful low tone of his voice and above all he was speaking with a northern German accent (my whole life I had only heard the southern accent from Bavaria and Baden-Württemberg that we spoke at home). "Please come!" he said to me.

I went in April 1981. My father was at the airport with flowers. He was 73 years old and I was 48. The apartment was filled with flowers from all the family and all his friends. Uncles, aunts and cousins were there, waiting. My father existed.... As with all absent fathers they exist but there is no real tie. I had only heard bad things about him all my life, which had increased my curiosity: I told myself that a person couldn't be that bad!" I was nurturing my need to know my "origins".

The Deichmann family originates from the region around the city of Bremen, from the small towns of Syke, Hoya, and Dörverden where grandfather Ivan was born. He married Rebecca Kahn from Luxembourg. For professional reasons they settled in Algrange, at the time called Algringen in German, in German occupied Lorraine. They opened a shop selling workmen's clothes. Their three children went to a German speaking primary school. After World War One, in 1918, the family was more or less given the choice of becoming French citizens, or leaving. They chose to remain German. In addition my paternal grandfather - and my maternal grandfather – had fought on the side of Germany during the First World War, which made them undesirable. They therefore returned to Syke.

Then the Nazis came into power and the day after "Crystal Night", 9 November 1938, all the Jewish men of Syke were arrested and interned in the Buchenwald concentration camp. Thanks to the intervention of my uncle Erich, the Brazilian consul of the region and the German consul in Rio, my grandfather stayed there eleven days. He was released on 22 November 1938 with an official letter and above all a visa to enter Brazil. In 1928 Erich, their eldest son, had gone to Brazil to join a cousin who had set up business in Rio at the turn of the 20th century. My paternal family's immigration to Brazil has been made possible through his intervention, and also because of the fact that war had not yet been declared.

My grandparents and their son Edgar succeeded in leaving Germany in December 1938. My father who was then in Belgium, sailed from Antwerp on 26 January 1939. His ship landed in Rio on 10 February 1939. He was 31 years old and had left his wife and daughter behind him. They arrived as impoverished foreign Jews speaking not a word of Portuguese: they were all settled in Resende, near Rio. It was an agricultural colony created by Baron de Hirsch; he had created the "Jewish Colonization Society" in 1891. He acquired a tract of land that he divided into smallholdings. My grandparents and their two youngest sons paid a minimum rent and spent the war years growing vegetables and raising chickens to survive. Erich, who was already a Brazilian citizen, sold their produce in Rio in order for them to have a little cash in addition to the little they had. The grandparents found it very difficult to adapt. My grandmother felt completely isolated on that farm in the countryside; she became severely depressed and wanted to commit suicide by throwing herself in the river... She had lost her belongings, and was now far away from the country of her birth, and from the other close members of her family, so dependent on her children. As for my father, he always said that his misfortune was to have been born Prussian! He felt totally out of step with Brazilian society, which was so much less structured than the one he had left behind.

Living conditions improved when they moved to Rio, where father opened a shop selling imported food items.

One day my grandmother, a very good cook, had made some German cakes and pastries for sale. My father's customers bought them and found them delicious. After a year some customers advised him to just make pastries, since they could buy the rest of the merchandise elsewhere. This is how his pastry shop was launched. Grandmother continued to bake cakes until her death in 1949. Then he recruited a German pastry chef who had been born in Brazil and some other staff, and "Confeitaria Kurt" was born. Despite the success, he wanted to remain small. His name was very well known in Rio.

From 1959 onwards my father lived in an apartment on the rua Alberto de Compos. His customers were his friends, they confided in him. He could have made a fortune, demand was growing, but he wanted to stay small "I didn't want to expand, I was afraid of myself " he confided to me, although I didn't quite understand what he meant. He just wanted to be able to live well and take a trip to Europe every summer. The clientele was essentially German, Jewish and non-Jewish. He wasn't overtly Jewish neither did he hide it. He was definitely not religious. His pastries were German and French: it was neutral!

Erich's business was manufacturing eyeglasses frames and Edgar opened a factory producing electrical components. When he retired he conducted many conferences back in his native region in Germany, on the fate of his family during the war. They all were a very hard working family. Culturally so German!

My cousin Evelyn now runs the pastry shop. She has – at last – brought in some chairs to turn it into a tearoom. On Jewish holidays, she sells special pastries like cakes without flower for Passover. For Christmas and Hanukkah the shop sells little pastries made of walnuts, figs and dried fruits, as well as the famous German "Stollen".

From the time I met my father, I had the feeling that I had a protector. I felt stronger, as if I had gained a support, a safety net, which continued even when he began to suffer from Alzheimer's disease. This feeling lasted from 1981 up until 23 February 2000, the day he died. A strange feeling emerged from the presence of a father who entered so late into my life. It is true that early childhood imprints are indelible.

One day I reproached him for having left us. He burst into tears. It was difficult to watch an old man cry and it had not been my intention to make him suffer for the past. In the years we spent together my father called me "Mein gutes", which is "darling" in German. My father did everything he could to make up for his absence. He must have lived with a deep sense of guilt

I was devastated when he died. It was the first time I had buried a member of my immediate family. Thinking of my mother, I could mourn my father.

I am so glad to have known Kurt ….

XV - Epilogue

During World War II I felt in constant danger of being taken away in a roundup, but I still went on with daily chores, I went on living... When we were standing in those endless lines, I didn't know if it was to register or to buy food. Since I was with my mother and she was everything to me, I felt protected.

Ever since my mother was taken away, I have felt a deep sense of guilt. She had died and not me. If we were to die, it should have been together. It would have been equally unbearable if I had died and not my mother; I was her reason for living. But in spite of my wish to always be with my mother, I felt relief that they hadn't taken me. There is a feeling of guilt that I have to live with. It emerges in everyday life, if something doesn't go well, I try right away to think of what I did wrong, that it is my fault. Then I try to rationalize.

Was my childhood stolen from me?

For eleven or twelve years, longer than the duration of the war, there was the period that I call "the time of the Nazis". Nazism dominated everything and I was prevented from living my life as a child, from discovering and experiencing life. From 1933 to 1945, as Jews, we were restricted in every way. This kind of enclosed period of my life enabled me to develop in other ways. Perhaps many other children who were not Jewish were confronted with similar problems, particularly if they had parents who were in the Resistance, or fathers who were prisoners of war.... Many children grew up without a father, and with no one providing a father figure. But they were not faced with life and death situations as I was although they did not grow up in a normal environment.

I should also mention that there were big divisions within my family. There were Nazi sympathizers on the protestant side of the family that remained in Germany. Certain members of that family, such as my cousin Kurt, crossed to the other side of the street when he met a Jewish aunt or uncle. This cousin's brother, Herbert, was killed on the Russian front. He was drafted into the Wehrmacht, to fight for Hitler, others died in Auschwitz, because of Hitler....

All her life my cousin Elisabeth has pressed me to take her to Paris. I never wanted to, because the idea of speaking German in Paris was unbearable. It reminded me too much of Nazi time. I spoke German with my family in Paris, but Elisabeth was too closely identified with Nazi occupied Paris. It has always been difficult for her to talk about the war with me. It has been much easier to do so with the younger generation of my German family.

There is a multicultural side to me, but I never lost my origins. I adapted and integrated to other cultures and they are also part of me.

My roots are German Jewish or Judeo-German, but I also belong to the French, American and, to a small extent, Swiss cultures: I am a truly multicultural hybrid. This enables me to feel at ease in many environments and belong to none or so multicultural that I belong to all. I thus feel rather like a potted plant, wherever I go, I take my roots along!

Concerning my mother's assassination, we found out in 1945 that she was not on any list of survivors, but only discovered in 1980 the details of convoy no. 12 that took her to Auschwitz. Before these dates very few people talked openly about the death camps. It was as late as 1997 that I was able to trace her whole journey to the gas chamber.

The details of my mother's life and death are in this book with all my memories of her, those of Elisabeth (the only family member alive today who knew her), many family photographs that I have collected over the years as well as official archives.

To help me mourn my mother, I tried to obtain an official death certificate from the French government, but their bureaucracy makes it impossible at this time. The Ministry responded in a letter saying that she "disappeared in Auschwitz and is presumed to be deceased". I now know that as soon as she stepped off the train she was led to the gas chamber without a serial number tattooed on her arm. No records were kept of those martyrs from convoy no. 12.

I think of my mother every day as she lives on beside me. How can you mourn someone who leaves the room, aged thirty-nine to disappear forever?

Since the end of the war I have always wished to write my mother's story. I want her name to remain unforgotten....

XVI - Addenda

1. The "Righteous of the Nations" title given to the Parignys.

Many years later, in August 2013 following the first edition of the French version of this book, I wanted to contact the Parignys again. They had left Normandy and my first attempt of finding their new residence failed. It was through the help of a friend that I was able to obtain their new address. They had moved to the South of France. Mme Parigny had died in the interim and so had the oldest son, Michel.

It was in August 2013 that Claudine, Daniel and I met again in Châteaurenard, a small town near Avignon, where they now reside. It was a great joy for all us.

In France 75% of the Jews had been saved from a likely death by very courageous citizens who defied the Nazi and Vichy regimes. M. and Mme Parigny were among those. When "Yad Vashem", the Shoah Martyrs' and Heroes' Remembrance Authority, was established by Israel's Knesset in 1952, a special tribute had been created to honor those who had saved Jews during World War II. These citizens were given the title of "Righteous of the Nations" which is Israel's highest civil award.

Upon my request to Yad Vashem giving proof that I was living with and thus had been saved by the Parigny family during the war, they were awarded posthumously the honorary title of "Righteous among the Nations" in late 2015. A "Righteous medal" bearing their names was made as well as a "Righteous Diploma".

A ceremony took place on 19 June 2016 in Châteaurenard's city hall in the presence of the mayor, the district's prefect, Israel's general consul and France's Yad Vashem' representative, along with a large public.

It was an extremely moving ceremony where all the official representatives, the family and myself gave a speech. Yad Vashem's representative gave the "Righteous of the Nations" Medal and Diploma to Claudine and Daniel Parigny in the presence of their children.

The names of François and Angèle Parigny will be engraved on the Wall of Honor in the Garden of the Righteous of the Nations at Yad Vashem in Jerusalem. Their names will also be engraved on a wall designed for the French "Righteous of the Nations", called "Les Justes" in French, outside of the Holocaust Museum in Paris.

2. A "Stolperstein" for my mother in 2016

"Stolperstein" means "Stumbling Block" in German. Gunter Demning, a German sculptor, initiated this art project in 1952. It is meant to be an individual memorial for Nazi victims, of which an overwhelming majority were Jews. They are funded and kept up by a group of citizens from the towns where they are laid.

A Stumbling Block is a cobblestone covered by a brass plate bearing the name, date and place of birth, date and place of the victim's "murder". They are then embedded into the sidewalk in front of the house were the victim resided before being persecuted by the Nazis. Most European Nazi occupied countries now honor their Jewish victims in such a way.

Recently there were two "Stolpersteine" laid for my mother: one in Karlsruhe, at 8bis Sudenstrasse, which was our last residence in Germany and one in Remich, Luxembourg, in front of the little house where we lived before fleeing to France.

I am hoping that one will be laid in Paris, my mother's very last residence before her death in Auschwitz.

3. Montréal, Canada with Hélène 2016-17

It was an immense surprise to receive in July 2016 a long letter from Hélène in Montreal. She wrote me that she had kept all my letters from 1946 to 1950, addressed to her mother and herself, approximately one hundred in all, and that she had given all of them to the The Quebec National Library and Archives, BAnQ, located in Montreal. It was then through the archivist, Mme Marthe Léger, that she was able to get in touch with me again!

Seventy years had passed! I was so terribly moved by reading all of those letters. It really felt like going back through a tunnel of time. The way I expressed myself then and the many details that I had forgotten! It was an amazing feeling, magical? I was reliving my life as a 14 year old girl in Paris and beyond in New York.

Until now I had never spoken to Hélène, much less seen her except on the few photographs we had exchanged. Because of my many moves back and forth across the Atlantic Ocean, I was unfortunately not able to keep any of her and her mother's letters except for the pictures and some trinkets that they had sent to me during those years.

Since last summer we have communicated by telephone. I now know the sound of her voice and the accent she speaks with, another very moving experience.

After all these years, we hope to meet in the near future.

We are both in our 85th year!

XVII - Annexes

1. History of the Jews of the Sarre region (Saarland) -

The first traces of Jewish families allowed to live in Homburg go back to 1330. In the early Christian era, the town was an important Celtic colony, then a roman city before being destroyed by the Alamans in 275 AD. Homburg owed its growth to its geographical situation at the axis of two important roads: from Strasbourg to Treves and Metz to Worms.

The Counts of Homburg, loyal vassals of the Emperor, are mentioned in 1172 as having their residence in the Castle de Melburg and then at Schlossberg. The fortress and the town were situated near an old military and trading route: a strategic crossroad between France and Germany. It was for that reason that in 1330 Emperor Louis of Bavaria conferred on the brothers the Counts Frédéric and Conrad de Homburg the rights and privileges of the town. Homburg was then in fact little more than a large village, and on the death of the last of the Counts, the town and the fortress reverted to the Counts of Nassau-Saarbrucken. The town enjoyed a brief period of growth at that time and the fortress was converted into a renaissance castle. Charles Quint accorded the town the right to hold a market, which was vital to its development.

In 1555, Pope Paul IV ordered that the Jews of the town be permitted to live only in one quarter of the town, the Ghetto. In 1750 the census noted 300 Jews in this Quarter.

The southern part of the Sarre region, Saarland, including Homburg, was annexed to France in 1661 and was subjected to the "Reuniting policy" of Louis IV.

Vauban, recognizing the strategic importance of the castle, transformed it into a stronghold between 1680 and 1692. A wall was built around the town. Then revolutionary France annexed the Sarre region and it became a department. It was given back to the Rhineland in 1815, only to be annexed again by France in 1918 when it was administered by the League of Nations for 15 years. On the expiration of the period it was reattached to the Reich in 1935, and then occupied again by France 1945.

On this political history is grafted the history of the Jews. They lived in this region since Roman times. After the Treaty of Verdun in 843, which dismantled the empire of Charlemagne, there developed a very hierarchical feudal society based on ownership of land. The Jews, excluded from living in the towns, could no longer be landowners and depended entirely on the emperor or on one of his vassals who could move or chase them away as they pleased. They were reduced to the status of serfs, living under vassals who proclaimed their own laws. Lords protected some to a greater or lesser extent, on the payment of high taxes. Others wandered the countryside, living a life of utmost misery. They were frequently the victims of pogroms and burned alive. In the Middle Ages, in particular at the time of the first crusade in the summer of 1096, all the Jewish communities of Lorraine and the Rhineland were destroyed.

It was in 1330 that began the history of the "utilization" of Jews in this region. Amongst the rights and privileges that towns enjoyed, were the right to "possess" and protect four Jewish families, on the payment of an admission's "fee" and an annual tax. Certain better off Jews, in the two senses of the term, were made "Hofschutzjuden" or court Jews.

On 13 November 1791, under Louis XVI, the "Jewish law" was promulgated, by which the Jews of France and the French territories including the Saarland, became full citizens.

On 20 July 1808, under Napoleon 1st, the Bayonne decree was issued, obliging all Jews to adopt a permanent family name. They had one month in which to do this and many retained their original names. This was the case for my ancestors the Arons.

2. The thirteen Bocks: the identity and fate of the children of a Judeo-Protestant couple

From around 1850 onwards there were many mixed marriages in Germany. My great grandmother, Elisabeth Wittmann, converted to Judaism before marrying my great grandfather in 1877 or 1878, but she retained a Christian upbringing and culture. In particular, I was told, she often sang protestant songs and lullabies to her children.

My great grandfather, Jacob Bock was not a religious Jew, but wanted to have a Jewish wedding. He had done his Bar Mitzvah and had been raised in a light and reformist Judaism.

The couple chose the man's religion, as was the practice of the time and they had 13 children who lived to become adults.

1. Léon, born in Munich. I don't know the religion he chose. He left for America very young and had three children, one of whom was Jeannette Bock, married name Lombard, who was a lovely lady. She and her husband came to visit us in Zurich in 1967. They live in Long Island, N.Y.
2. Bertha, my grandmother, born in Munich 12 January 1880 and died in London 13 July 1973. She had four children (whose lives are recounted in this book).
3. Sophie Schutt, born in Furth, 2 December 1882. The photos show her to be beautiful. Married a Protestant and practiced the Christian religion. Despite that fact, she was

arrested as a Jew in Munich in a roundup and shot in Kaunas, Lithuania, 25 November 1941. No children.
4. Jenny, Jewish also married a Jew, M. Midas. She was also shot in Kaunas, Lithuania, 25 November 1941.
5. Jules. Not religious at all, had racehorses in Furth. Married a Jew very late in life in New York. No children.
6. Karl, born 10 June 1887, married a Jew. He died 5 July 1943 in New York. No children.
7. Mili (whose name must have been Emilie) born 1885 and died 1964 in Furth. She was the one who brought us together, was always in touch with her siblings. She had three children and her daughter continued in this role.
8. Ida, born 6 September 1888 in Furth, died 2 November 1970 in New York. No children.
9. Elisabeth called Betty, born 9 November 1893, died 8 October 1953. Christian, even converted to Catholicism. No children. She was a schoolteacher at a technical high school and was very religious.
10. Richard, born in 1896, died in Nurnberg. He was protestant and married to a protestant. No children.
11. Frieda (we called her Fridl) born 22 February 1899 died in Nurnberg 31 December 1973. She was Protestant, married and then divorced from M. Brandl, fighter pilot, member of the Nazi party. He did not want to be married to a half-Jew any more. She was beautiful and attracted men right up to the end of her life. She lived in Manhattan with her sister Ida, her opposite in every way!
12. Ernest, born around 1901, married a Jew. Died by firing squad at Kaunas, Lithuania 25 November 1941 with his wife and daughter Erika.
13. Théodor, born around 1901, handsome, no doubt felt Jewish but was not practicing. Died in New York of cancer of the tongue. He worked in a factory producing watch frames and had to lick a brush dipped in a radium solution. Had a girlfriend, no children.

How did they earn their living? What were their trades/occupations?

The men were all in commerce: businessmen, salesmen, wholesalers, shop workers or owners.

The women were mostly housewives, except for Jenny who was a nurse, Ida who was a personnel assistant and Betty who was a teacher.

How can we explain their diverse religious development?

They made their choices by identifying with their father or their mother, or through marriages and personal decisions. They concealed their Protestant roots or their Jewish roots. It was more about belonging than about religious practice for the most part. There were more Jewish men than Jewish women. We note one divorce, for reason of race.

I have photos of most of their tombs, which helped me draw up this list.

In my line of the family tree, after the death of my grandfather Isidor, the religious Jew of the family, no one practiced the Jewish religion. Apart from a few, they remained the "three day Jews" who only celebrated the three main Holidays, or even only one: Yum Kippur!

My mother, in Luxembourg, combined the Jewish and the Christian religious holidays. For example Christmas and Hanukkah were linked.

How does one explain so few descendants?

The thirteen Bock children had very few children. Is it because they did not enjoy being born into such a very large family? A baby seems to have been born every two or three years from 1881 to 1901. I was told that many blamed their father, whom they held responsible for the large number of children!

3. Comparative history

Historical parallels	Political events in the countries concerned by my family	My family
30 January 1933	Hitler appointed Chancellor.	I was born on November 18, 1932. My life, and that of my family until 1945 and beyond, was affected by the Nazis.
1 April 1933	Boycott of all Jewish businesses and Jewish professionals.	My grandfather's business is affected, as are all the others. That day is the signal that all Jews will be excluded from Germany's economy.
7 April 1933	Laws are promulgated to exclude Jews from civil service jobs, in the fields of law, medicine, journalism and culture in general.	Between 1933 and 1938, laws forced the Jews to sell all their businesses to Aryans.
11 April 1933	Definition of a "non Aryan": anyone who has a Jewish parent or grandparent. This will be included in the Nurnberg racial laws of September 1935.	
April 1934		My parents and I move to Luxembourg (Remich).
18 January 1935	The Sarre region is reattached to Germany.	
15 Sept. 1935 and 14 Nov. 1935	The Nurnberg racial laws are promulgated. German Jews lose their nationality.	From that day on we all became stateless. Jews are isolated, ostracized and confronted with violence and poverty.
2 March 1938		My grandfather dies of cancer in Saarbrucken.
24 April 1938	Jews must declare all their belongings that are worth over 5,000 Marks.	
Summer of 1938		My mother and I move to Luxembourg city. I start Kindergarten.

6 July 1938	The international conference held in Evian, France, was a failure. The whole world is witness to the Nazi persecutions, but is not moved by them. The borders are closing like a trap on the Jews.	
July and August 1938	Some Synagogues were beginning to be destroyed.	37 000 out of 500 000 Jews leave Germany.
17 August 1938	On all German Jew passports the first name is preceded by "Israel" for the men and "Sarah" for the women.	This is the case for the members of my family who have a passport.
5 Oct. 1938	In addition to the above and upon the request of the Swiss gov't, a large "J" either in red or black, is stamped on the front page of the passports.	Jews in Nazi Germany were very conscious that to stay was at the peril of their lives. Some emigrated very early.
9 - 10 Nov. 1938	On "Crystal Night" 267 synagogues were destroyed. Jews were killed or deported to the camps of Dachau, Buchenwald or Sachsenhausen.	My paternal grandfather. Ivan Deichmann, was arrested and deported to Buchenwald on 10 November
Early 1939		After my grandfather's death, my grandmother wanted to join her son in Paris. Uncle Paul worked and lived in Paris since 1934. She puts her household goods in storage. All is stolen or sold shortly thereafter.
3 Sept. 1939	Great Britain and France declare war on Germany. It is the beginning of World War II.	I start primary school in Luxembourg city.
18 March 1940		My mother received a letter from the gov't stating that we had to leave Luxembourg within 2 months.
10 May 1940	German troops invade Luxembourg.	
20 May 1940	Opening of Auschwitz concentration camp in Poland.	
10 June 1940	German troops invade France.	
22 June 1940	Armistice is signed in France. The country is divided in two.	

	The North is under the Nazi regime and the South is directed by Petain's Vichy gov't.	
End of August 1940		My mother and I illegally enter France hidden in a truck.
12 Sept. 1940	All the Jews are officially forced to leave Luxembourg.	We live in Paris.
15 Sept. 1940	Between September 1940 and 1942, the Vichy gov't shows supports for German anti-Jewish laws and deports a greater number of Jews than requested by the Nazis.	We move to 12, rue Caffarelli in Paris. I attend the nearby primary school rue Beranger.
27 Sept. 1940	1st anti-Jewish decree in France's occupied zone. Every Jew must go and register at the local City Hall. This will become the infamous "family records" used in the mass roundups.	
6 Oct. 1940	The registration is done by alphabetical order, names beginning with the letter "D" is on that day.	My mother registers herself as "head of family" and my name is entered as dependent.
29 March 1941	A special Vichy gov't department is opened. Its sole function concerns the Jews in France.	
Oct. 1941	A special police is formed whose duty is to track and arrest Jews.	
11 Dec. 1941	The USA declare war on Germany and Japan	
20 January 1942	The Wannsee conference held in Berlin, high Nazi officials plan the details for the destruction of European Jews, called the "Final solution".	We are tracked and even more impoverished.
7 Feb. 1942	6- decree forbids the Jews to leave their home between 8 p.m. and 6 a.m.	Through forgetfulness I stayed out one day beyond the limit.

7 June 1942	8th anti-Jewish decree. Every Jew from age 6 and up has to	I never go out without my "Star".

	wear a yellow star of David made out of cloth with the word "Jew" written on it and sewn on the lapel.	
8 July 1942	9th decree forbids the Jews to attend all public places and parks, theaters or movies. The are only allowed to do their shopping between 3 and 4 p.m.	We are grounded at home.
16 July 1942	Day 1 of the massive roundup: called the "Rafle du Vel d'hiv".	My mother is arrested and interned in Drancy.
17 July 1942	Day 2 of the roundup.	Grandmother and I go into hiding.
29 July 1942	Convoy no.12 leaves Drancy by freight train for the Auschwitz death camp.	My mother is in one of the railroad cars. It takes 60 hours to reach Auschwitz.
31 July 1942	My mother arrives in Auschwitz.	In getting off the train my mother is directed towards the gas chamber and murdered with Zyklon B gas.
6 June 1944	Allied forces landed in Normandy – D-Day.	We have to leave St Hilaire du Harcouët.
14 June 1944	Bombardment and destruction of St-Hilaire-du-Harcouët.	
July 44	Liberation of St-Hilaire-du-Harcouët.	We return to a house in ruins
Dec. 1944	The allies liberate Paris in August 44.	I return to Paris with uncle Paul. We are reunited with grandmother.
8 May 1945	The Nazis capitulate. It is the end of WW II in Europe.	

XVIII - Bibliography

Journal, Hélène Berr, Tallandier, 2008.

Juden in Homburg, Dieter Blinn, Ermer, 1993.

Chère Mademoiselle, Patrick Cabanel, Calmann-Lévy, 2010.

Ô Vous, frères humains, Albert Cohen, Gallimard, 1972.

Traqués, Cachés, Vivants, Collectif, L'Harmattan, 2004.

L'Occupation allemande en France, Jean Defrasne, P.U.F., 1985.

A Genius of war, Carlo D'Este, Harper Collins, 1995.

Aucun de Nous ne reviendra, Charlotte Delbo, Minuit, 1995.

L'Allemagne nazie et les juifs I, Saul Friedländer, Seuil, 1997.

La Destruction des juifs d'Europe I, Raul Hilberg, Gallimard, 1985.

Le Fichier, Annette Kahn, Robert Laffont, 1993

Les Juifs pendant l'occupation, André Kaspi, Seuil, 1991 et 1997.

Le Calendrier, Serge Klarsfeld, Fils et filles de déportés juifs de France – F.F.D.J.F., 1993.

L'étoile des juifs, Serge Klarsfeld, l'Archipel 1992.

Vichy-Auschwitz I, Serge Klarsfeld, Fayard, 1983. L'Etoile des juifs, Serge Klarsfeld, l'Archipel, 1992.

Si C'est un homme, Primo Levi, Julliard, 1987.

Rapport sur Auschwitz, Primo Levi, Kimé, 2005.

La Grande rafle du Vel d'Hiv, Claude Lévy et Paul Tillard, Robert Laffont, 1992.

La Rafle du Vel d'hiv, Maurice Rajsfus, P.U.F., 2002.

Les Juifs sous l'Occupation, Recueil des textes officiels français et allemands 1940-1944, Fils et filles de déportés juifs de France – F.F.D.J.F., 1982.

Le Fichier juif, René Rémond, Plon, 1996.

Les Normands sous l'occupation, Thibault Richard, Charles Corlet, 1998.

Retour sur la question juive, Élisabeth Roudinesco, Albin Michel, 2009.

« Assassinat d'une modiste », un film documentaire de Catherine Bernstein. Coproduction : ARTE France, IO Production (2005).